Vincent Perronet

Some Reflections by Way of Dialogue

On the Nature of Original Sin, Baptismal Regeneration, Repentance....

Vincent Perronet

Some Reflections by Way of Dialogue
On the Nature of Original Sin, Baptismal Regeneration, Repentance....

ISBN/EAN: 9783337184346

Printed in Europe, USA, Canada, Australia, Japan

Cover: Foto ©Lupo / pixelio.de

More available books at **www.hansebooks.com**

SOME REFLECTIONS,

By way of DIALOGUE,

On the NATURE of

Original Sin, Baptismal Regeneration, Repentance, the *New Birth, Faith, Justification, Christian Perfection,* or *Universal Holiness,* and the *Inspiration* of the *Spirit* of GOD.

Ἡμεῖς δὲ κηρύσσομεν Χριστὸν ἐσταυρωμένον, Ἰουδαίοις μὲν σκάνδαλον, Ἕλλησι δὲ μωρίαν.   1 Cor. i. 23.

—σὺ τί λέγεις, ὦ Ἕλλην; σοφίαν ζητεῖς; Ἔχεις τὸν Χριστὸν, σοφίαν ὄντα τοῦ Πατρός. Οἱ μὲν γὰρ φιλόσοφοι περὶ ψυχρὰ κỳ ἀνόνητα ἠσχολήθησαν· ὁ δὲ σταυρὸς τὸν κόσμον ἔσωσε.   Theophyl. in 1 Cor. i. 24, 25.

Νέκρωσον τοίνυν τὸ σῶμα, ἵνα οἰκῇ τὸ πνεῦμα ἐν σοί, καὶ δι᾽ αὐτὸ δοθῇ σοι ἡ ζωή.   Idem, in Rom. viii. 11.

Humbly Inscribed to the Most Reverend and Right Reverend the Lords the Archbishops, and Bishops of ENGLAND.

The FIFTH EDITION, with an APPENDIX.

By VIN. PERRONET, A.M.
Vicar of *Shoreham* in *Kent,* and
Chaplain to the Right Honourable Earl STANHOPE.

LONDON:
Printed and Sold by J. and W. OLIVER, in Bartholomew-Close near West-Smithfield. 1767.

TO THE

Most Reverend and Right Reverend

The LORDS the

ARCHBISHOPS and BISHOPS

OF

ENGLAND.

MY LORDS,

THough the Obscurity of the Author cannot challenge the Honour he thus ventures to assume to himself; yet the great and important Doctrines here treated of, both of the *sacred Writ-*

DEDICATION.

ings, and of our *own Church*, will sufficiently plead his Excuse. And indeed, as your Lordships ought to be esteemed principal Guardians of such Doctrines; therefore the Patronage of them, so far as they appear to be *such*, must, in part at least, belong to your Lordships.

That *Justification by Faith*, which is one of the Doctrines here explained, has been variously understood, cannot, my Lords, be a Secret to you: But this can neither lessen the Truth, nor the Importance of it.

That it is a Doctrine of our own Church, none will venture to deny; though by the cold manner in which it is sometimes treated, one would go near to suspect, that some Gentlemen were quite tired of it.

It may certainly, my Lords, be asked, whether Men are always to hold Opinions,

DEDICATION.

ons, which cannot be defended by the *Gospel*; because they were once espoused by the *Church*?

My Lords, They who have a due Regard for the divine Authority of the Gospel, or for the *Principles* of the *Reformation*, cannot long be in Suspense about answering such a Question.

However, my Lords, till this really appears to be the Case of any of our Doctrines, it is in Charity to be hoped, that no Member of our excellent Church will either be ashamed of her Doctrines, or afraid to espouse them; lest he only prove *ashamed of the Gospel of* Christ.

How far, my Lords, the Agreement is here shewn between an *antiquated* Doctrine or two of our own Church, and that divine Gospel: And how far some dangerous and fatal Errors are laid open, which strike at the very Foun-

DEDICATION.

dations of *Christianity*;--These are Points, which are humbly submitted to the unprejudiced Judgments of your Lordships, as well as to that of every other serious and wise Christian.—I am, with the greatest Deference and Respect,

My Lords,

Your Lordships

most dutiful Son,

and Servant,

VIN. PERRONET.

THE PREFACE.

WHAT *awful* Words are these! "If our *GOSPEL* be *hid*, it is *hid* to them that are *lost*; in whom the *God of this World* hath *blinded* the Minds of them which *believe not*; lest the *Light* of the glorious *GOSPEL* of *CHRIST*, who is the Image of God, should *shine* unto them (*a*)."

Miserable, undone Souls! The *Light*, the *Truth*, the *divine Excellency* of the *GOSPEL* hid from them!

Thus the Almighty makes good his righteous Threatning; "because they "received not the *Love* of the *Truth*, "that they might be saved; for this "Cause God shall send them strong "*Delusion*, that they should believe a "*Lye* (*b*)."—How *melancholy*, how *deplorable* a State, to be thus deserted of God, and his divine Grace!

May the Lord set these Reflections so home upon the Heart of every proud and obstinate *Infidel*, that he may find no Rest, till he is *pluckt as a Brand out of the Fire!*—But now, what shall we say of those

(*a*) 2 Cor. iv. 3, 4.
(*b*) 2 Thess. ii. 10—12.

THE PREFACE.

those miserable *Professors of Christianity*, who may have largely contributed to the *Sin* and *Ruin* of those immortal Souls, by being a *Scandal* and *Reproach* to the Profession of the *Gospel?*--"It must needs be, says the blessed *Jesus*, that Offences come; but *Wo* to that Man by whom the Offence cometh (*a*)!"

Various Ways have those, who are called *Christians*, dishonoured the *Christian* Name.

Some, by Vices, which would even shock a sober *Heathen*.---Some, by an *uncharitable, furious,* and *intolerant* Spirit.--- Some, by an eager Pursuit after the *Pleasures,* or *Riches,* or *Honours* of Life. Surely, neither the *sensual,* the *lewd,* the *proud,* the *vain,* the *covetous,* nor the *ambitious* Christian, can ever bring *much Honour* to the Religion of a *crucified Jesus!* A Religion, which injoins us *Mortification,* and *Self-denial; Purity of Heart,* and *Holiness of Conversation;* a *lowly, humble, heavenly* Mind; not to *love the World,* nor to be *conformed* to it; but to *set our Affections on Things above, not on Things on the Earth!*

Therefore, when the Enemies of *Christianity* (who are *sharp-sighted* enough in
every

(*a*) St Matth. xviii. 7.

every Thing, but what concerns their *eternal Salvation*; when these) observe too many *Professors* of the *Gospel* thus *trifling* with it, can it be any Wonder that *Infidelity* gains Ground in the World? I presume it cannot. — For *Infidelity*, I am persuaded, will always gain Strength in Proportion as the Gospel loses its *divine Efficacy* on the Hearts and Minds of its *Professors*.

Let this *divine Efficacy* but shine forth in its *full Lustre*,—and *Infidelity* will lose its *strongest Hold*. For though the *God of this World* found Means to *blind* Mankind, even in the purest Times of the *Gospel*; yet it may be submitted, whether the *Lives* of *Christians* have not too long furnished him with his most *dangerous* and formidable *Weapons?*—Could *Reason* and *Argument* have disarmed him, he had been long since *disarmed*;—but *something else* is wanting.

However, it must be the Duty of every one, according to his *Station, Circumstances,* and *Abilities,* to endeavour to enforce the *Gospel* upon the Hearts of Men. — But which is the most promising Method to succeed? Is it not to propose it in its *native Simplicity?* This surely must be the most likely Way to bring
down

down a *Blessing* upon our Endeavours. For though to accommodate its *Doctrines* either to the *Prejudices* of *Philosophers*; or to the *Taste* of a *giddy, thoughtless* and *sceptical* Age, might please some *refined Reasoners*; as well as a *Multitude* of others, who cannot relish a Religion which proposes a *Cross* and a *narrow Way*; yet this would be only betraying *their* Souls, and murdering of our *own*; though we might thus effectually escape the usual Charge of *Enthusiasm*.

I have therefore endeavoured, in the following *Dialogue*, to give a *plain* Account of some fundamental Doctrines of the *Gospel* of *Christ*, without knowingly departing from it, either on the Right Hand, or on the Left.

Indeed it will appear, that I differ in some Measure from the late learned and worthy *Bishop* of *London* (*a*), in relation to the " *Spirit bearing witness with our Spi-* " *rit that we are the Children of God:*" Yet I hope it is done in such a Manner, as could not give the least Offence, either to his Lordship, or any other truly wise and serious *Christian*.

His

(*a*) See his Lordship's *Discourses* preached at the *Temple*, *Discourse* the *Eighth*.

His Lordſhip has certainly proved, with great Strength of Reaſon, that there muſt be *Two* who *bear witneſs*; " and " that thoſe *Two* are the *Holy Spirit of* " *God*, and our *own Spirit:*" Yet I muſt beg leave to enter my Diſſent, where his Lordſhip denies " the Evidence of the " Spirit to be *any* ſecret Inſpiration, or " *any* Aſſurance conveyed to the Mind " of the Faithful;" but intirely confines it to " the *Evidence* of *ſuch Works* " as we perform by the Spirit," P. 247.

However, as at the Entrance of that *Diſcourſe*, the *Sentiments* of that learned *Prelate* are ſo very juſt, and withal ſo very *different* from thoſe of many *Moderns*, I can't avoid tranſcribing a Part of what is there mentioned.

His Lordſhip obſerves, that " to be
" the *Children of God* is the greateſt Privi-
" lege under the *Goſpel*:—And as this is
" a *New State*, which belongs not to us
" by *Nature*; ſo our Entrance into it is
" ſtiled a *New Birth*; and we are ſaid
" *to be born again*, and *to be begotten again*,
" to the Hopes [of the Goſpel]—And
" therefore as we receive our *Spiritual*
" *Life from* the Gift and Mercy of God,
" he is our Father, and we are his
Children.

"Children. Thus St *Peter* tells us, that *we are born again, not of corruptible Seed, but of incorruptible, by the Word of God, which liveth and abideth for ever.*" 1 Epiftle i. 23.

"This *new Life* we receive by the Miniftration of the *Spirit*: The *Powers* which belong to *this Life*, and in which it confifts, depend upon the *Influences* of the *Spirit*; and therefore we are faid *to be born of the Spirit*. He is the *Earneft* of our Inheritance; the *Pledge* and *Security* which we receive from God of our future Immortality." Page 227, 228.

I fhall here only juft enquire —Whether from this beautiful Account of our *Spiritual Life*; of the *new Birth*, and the *Powers* belonging to it; of the *Miniftration, Influences,* and divine *Offices* of the *Holy Spirit*, a Perfon would not naturally conclude, that the *Power of knowing we are the Children of God*, muft alfo proceed from fome *divine Influence* or *Operation* upon the Soul (*a*)?

(*a*) See Page 88. of the following *Dialogue*, Note (*b*).

SOME

POSTSCRIPT.

SOME FEW REFLECTIONS

ON A

FUTURE STATE of THINGS;

Humbly offered to the serious Consideration of such MODERNS as disbelieve the IMMORTALITY of the SOUL.

I. IS not the most consummate *Happiness* worth seeking after?

II. Is not the most consummate *Misery* worth avoiding?

III. Must not the one or the other be our Portion hereafter, if the *Gospel* be *true*?

IV. But what if the *Gospel* be *false*?

V. Why then, it must be allowed, that a *true Christian is sadly* disappointed! — However, let us examine, what *Hurt* the *Belief* of a glorious *Immortality* has done him?

VI. We

POSTSCRIPT.

VI. We will admit, that this *Belief* has robbed him of many *irregular Gratifications*; deprived him of many *fashionable Vices*; restrained many *craving Appetites*; curbed many *violent Passions*; subdued many *darling Desires*; nay hindered him of all those *worldly Possessions*, which he could not enjoy with a *good Conscience*; and perhaps exposed him to the *Laughter* and *Ridicule* of a *gay World*; of many *Free-thinkers* and *Free-livers*.—All this we will suppose he has suffered for his *Hopes* of *Immortality*.

VII. But are these *Hopes* really worth all these *Sufferings?*

VIII. Let us fairly examine.— In general then, these *Hopes* have been a continual *Feast* to his Mind; and have constantly furnished out such inconceivable *Joy* and *Happiness*, as he would not have exchanged for the Possession of the whole World! Were they therefore not worth the whole World to *Him*; and even this upon the Supposition that his *Hopes* were ill-founded?

IX. But let us proceed next to enquire, how Matters stand with those Gentlemen who scorn to indulge any *Hopes* of this kind?

X. First, It must be granted, that as they have shook off all the *Shackles* of *Religion*, they certainly enjoy a *Freedom*, which the poor *Believer* does not. Therefore, as they are
under

POSTSCRIPT.

under none of those *slavish Restraints*, they are at full *Liberty* to give a complete *Swing* to their *Passions* and *Pleasures*; to their *Pride, Ambition*, and *Revenge*.

XI. However, by way of *Counter-balance*, may not this *free Indulgence* sometimes cost them pretty dear? May it not prove to the Loss of their *Reputations*, their *Peace*, their *Health*, their *Estates*, and perhaps their *Lives*?

XII. But let us view these Gentlemen in the most *advantageous* Light.—Let us suppose they have so much *Philosophy* and *Prudence*, and Command of their *Passions*, that they are not *Slaves* to their *Appetites*; but that they avoid every *outward Vice* of the Age; and thus maintain a *fair Reputation*, and a *sound Body*:—Yet it is most evident, that notwithstanding they do not live the *Life* of a *Beast*, yet their highest Expectations are only to die the *Death* of a *Beast!*

XIII. Therefore, supposing there was nothing beyond the *Grave*; yet as such Persons deprive themselves of a present unspeakable *Happiness* arising from the *Hopes* of a glorious *Immortality*;—it cannot be, but they must certainly have the *Disadvantage*. So just and beautiful are the Sentiments of that ancient *Philosopher*, who declared,—" That if the " *Belief* of the *Soul's Immortality* was a *Mis-* " *take*; it was however so *delightful* a Mistake,

B 2 " that

"that he would not suffer himself to be rob-
"bed of it, as long as he lived! *"

XIV. But can the *gloomy Prospect* of sinking into *Nothing* afford this *Pleasure?* — What a dreadful *Gloom* must possess that *Mind* which can believe it? — And what malicious *Dæmon* must possess that *Man*, who would deprive others of their *Hopes* of *Immortality?*

XV. And now, to finish this *Address*, let us do common Justice to the *Gospel*. — We have hitherto reasoned upon a Supposition, that the *Gospel* gave us a *false* Account of *Immortality*. Let us now for Argument's Sake, suppose the *Gospel* is *true:* — Who then is the *wise* Man? — Is it he that has enjoyed during his whole Life, the *reviving*, *lovely* Prospect of *endless Happiness*; and which he will one Day enter upon? Or is it he that has deprived himself of that *divine Pleasure* in this World, and whose Portion is a *dreadful Scene* of *Misery* in the other?

---

* Quòd si in hoc erro, quòd Animos hominum immortales esse credam, lubenter erro : nec mihi hunc errorem, quo delector, dum vivo, extorqueri volo.
M. T. CICERO, *de Senect.*

SOME

SOME REFLECTIONS,

By way of DIALOGUE, &c.

BETWEEN

PHILALETHES and EUGENIUS.

Eugenius.

I Have often thought, my dear Friend, that *eternal Salvation* is a very weighty Affair; and therefore have been very desirous to know, *What I must do to be saved?*

Phil. It is a little unusual, my worthy Friend *Eugenius*, to see a Person of Birth and Fortune, especially of your Years, making so *unfashionable* an Enquiry. But when once the Spirit of God has effectually touched the Heart, neither Youth, nor Riches, nor Honours, can withstand the powerful Influence.

E. I have various Questions to trouble you with; but desire to be first informed, What is to be understood by *Original Sin?* For I think

think a learned *Lutheran* talks of no lefs than fixteen Opinions about it (*a*).

P. You certainly begin with a very proper Queftion: For till we know the true Foundation of our fpiritual Diforders, we fhall hardly be able to get rid of them. The Variety of Opinions concerning *Original Sin,* or any other Doctrine whatever, will have no other Effect on a wife and good Mind, than to make it the more careful in diftinguifhing Truth from Falfhood. It is commonly faid of our learned and excellent *Cudworth,* that, in his *Intellectual Syftem,* he had *raifed more Spirits than he could lay:* And fuppofing this to be fo; yet his Subject is not the lefs *True,* the lefs *Weighty,* or the lefs *Important.* So that, admitting there were many more Opinions about *Original Sin,* we have no further Concern with them, than only to endeavour to fix upon the right: And fince I cannot help you to a better, than that of our own Church, be pleafed to hear what that is.— *Original Sin,* according to her, " is the Cor-
" ruption of every Man's Nature; whereby
" he is very far gone from original Righte-
" oufnefs; and is of his own Nature inclined
" to Evil: And which Corruption deferves
" God's Wrath, *&c.*"

This is, in brief, what our Church fays (*b*): And I think, as the *Scripture* fpeaks much

to

(*a*) *Ofiander* in Bifhop *Taylor's* Polemical Difcourfes, page 452.
(*b*) Article IX.

to the same Purpose (*a*); so the unhappy Experience of Mankind will vouch for no small Part of it.—There is not, perhaps, any thing in divine Revelation, to which proud Reason stoops more unwillingly: And therefore it has found out numberless Glosses and Comments, rather than submit to a mortifying Doctrine, which represents all Mankind as a Race of *degenerate, fallen* Spirits.

E. Some, I know, have thought, that the Doctrine of *Original Sin* bears hard upon Divine Goodness.

P. Undoubtedly it does, as it has sometimes been explained. But if God has abundantly made up our original Loss; if, *where Sin abounded*, there *Grace did much more abound* (*b*), then every Divine Attribute remains safe and untouched. Perhaps indeed Mankind may not be able to comprehend the *Reason*, why infinite Wisdom should choose rather amply to repair that Loss, than to prevent it at first:—And if this be the Cause of our Unbelief, let us modestly remember, that *we are but of Yesterday*, and know nothing (*c*). That illustrious *Heathen, Socrates,* gained the Name of the wisest Man, by forming very humble Conceptions of *human Wisdom*, in general; and

---

(*a*) Gen. i 26, 27. Ch. ii. 17. Ch. iii. Psalm li. 5. Eccles. vii. 29. Rom. iii. 9, 19, 23. Ch. v. 6—21. Ch. vi. 23. Ch. vii. 14—25. Ch. viii. 6—8. 2 Cor. v. 14. Gal. iii. 22. Ephes. ii. 3. Ch. iv. 22—24. See also St John iii. 3—8. St Pet. i. 3, 4, 23. 1 St John iii. 9. Ch. v. 4, 18.

(*b*) Rom. v. 15—21.   (*c*) Job viii. 9.

and of his *own* in particular (*a*). But he that *will* know the Reasons of God's Dispensations, *before* he believes them, has neither the *Wisdom* of that Philosopher, nor the *Modesty* of a *Christian.*

I am not contending, my good Friend, for a *blind, popish* Faith, which *implicitly* submits itself to *Man*, or the *Church:* But when we have sufficient Reason to believe the Voice to be the Voice of God, there the Understanding ought to pay an entire and absolute Submission: And when once the Meaning of that Voice is clear to us, there is then left no room for disputing; but we ought rather to *hide ourselves in the Dust* (*b*), and to receive it with the deepest Humility.

Let us now hear the Sentiments of a great Master of Reasoning, who was never charged with *Bigotry* or *Enthusiasm.* —— " There is
" one sort of Propositions, that challenge the
" *highest* Degree of our Assent upon *bare Testimony*;
" whether the Thing proposed agree
" or disagree with common Experience, and
" the ordinary Course of Things, or no. The
" Reason whereof is, because the Testimony
" is of such a One as cannot deceive, nor be
" deceived, and that is, of God himself. This
" carries with it *Certainty* beyond *Doubt*, *Evidence*
" beyond *Exception*. This is called
" by a peculiar Name, *Revelation*; and our
" Assent

(*a*) — Τῷ ὄντι ὁ θεὸς σοφὸς εἶναι — ἡ ἀνθρωπίνη σοφία ὀλίγε τινὸς ἀξία ἐστὶ κ̑ οὐδενός. Plat. Apol. Socrat.

(*b*) Isai. ii. 10, 11.

"Assent to it, *Faith*; which as absolutely determines our Minds, as our *Knowledge* itself; and we may as well doubt of our own Being, as we can, whether *any Revelation* from God be true. So that *Faith* is a settled and sure Principle of Assent and Assurance, and leaves no manner of room for *Doubt* or *Hesitation* —*Faith* is nothing else but an Assent founded on the *biggest Reason.* —*Reason* is not injured or disturbed, but assisted and improved, by new Discoveries of Truth, coming from the eternal Fountain of all Knowledge.——Whatsoever is divine Revelation, ought to over-rule all our *Opinions, Prejudices,* and *Interests,* and hath a Right to be received with a *full Assent.*" *Locke*'s *Human Understanding,* B. iv. C. 16. §. 14. C. 18. §. 10.

E. I so far entirely agree with that great Man. But is not *Baptism,* in the Opinion of our Church, a *spiritual Regeneration*; by which, though we are *born in Sin, and the Children of Wrath,* we are *made Members of Christ, Children of God, and Inheritors of the Kingdom of Heaven* (a)?

P. It is as you say. And our Church means by all this, that we have hereby a Title and Claim, through the Blood of *Christ,* to eternal Happiness: And which we shall certainly enjoy, if we continue faithful to our *Baptismal Covenant.*—But then, as we expect this, we are

(a) Office for *Baptism,* and the *Church Catechism*; and Art. 27.

are obliged, when grown up, "to *crucify* the "old Man, and *utterly* to abolish the whole "Body of Sin; to follow the *Example* of our "Saviour *Christ*, and to be made *like* unto him; "that as he died and rose again for us, so "should we who are baptized, *die from Sin*, "and *rise again unto Righteousness, continually* "mortifying *all our evil and corrupt Affections*; "and *daily* proceeding in *all* Virtue and God- "liness of living (*a*)."

You see then, my dear *Eugenius*, what is the *constant* Task of a *Christian*, if he designs to be the better for his *Baptism*.

E. I see it very plainly. And withal, that, according to our Church, there is a *Body of Sin* remaining *after* Baptism; and consequently, that the Corruption of our Nature is not taken away by it.

P. That it is not, our Church expressly affirms (*b*): And our own Experience may abundantly convince us.—But it is against this Corruption, and all the Sins which flow from it, that we are daily to strive and petition. And God's holy Spirit, if it be not our own Fault, will give us the Victory (*c*). But we must,

(*a*) See the last Prayer in the Office of *Baptism*; and the Exhortation that follows it.

(*b*) Article IX. Whoever compares the *English* with the *Latin* Article, will easily perceive, that by *regenerated* is *there* meant *baptized*. However we shall plainly see, that our *Church* means also something else by *Regeneration*, than merely *Baptism*.

(*c*) Rom. vi. 6, 11—15, 22. 1 Cor. xv. 56, 57. I must here observe, that with regard to these Words,—
"God's

muſt, my Friend, uſe great Diligence and Watchfulneſs; be often in Prayer, and never wilfully neglect any *Means* of Grace whatever (*a*). And then we need not doubt, but *the Blood of Jeſus Chriſt will cleanſe us from all Sin* (*b*).

E. I ſhould be glad to be informed, whether St *Paul* ſpeaks of himſelf, or of ſome other Perſon, in thoſe remarkable Words, in the ſeventh of the *Romans*,—*I am carnal, ſold under Sin.*—*I ſee another Law in my Members, bringing me into Captivity to the Law of Sin.*—*O wretched Man that I am, who ſhall deliver me from the Body of this Death?*—*With the Mind, I myſelf ſerve the Law of God; but with the Fleſh, the Law of Sin* (*c*).

I muſt own, it was not diſagreeable to me, to ſuppoſe that the Apoſtle ſpake of himſelf; becauſe I thought, that, if ſo extraordinary a

Perſon

"God's *Holy Spirit*, if it be not our own Fault, will give us the Victory;—— a certain learned Gentleman thus objected:—" Here, ſays he, the Point turns on the *Will* of Man; which in P. 1. is wholly aſcribed to the *Power of God's Work* on the Soul."——If other Readers ſhould make the ſame Objection, I deſire they would reflect, that what is mentioned, P. 1. relates to thoſe *firſt ſtrong Convictions*, which often, in a powerful manner, carry all before them: Whereas the other Paſſage relates to thoſe *gentle Workings* of the *Spirit*, which are too often hindered by our own wilful Follies —— See Ephes. iv. 30. Phil. ii. 12, 13. 1 Theſſ. v. 19. 2 St Pet. i. 5—11.——This alſo will ſolve the very ſame Objection which was likewiſe made to Part of P. 21.

(*a*) St Matth. xxvi. 41. St Luke xi. 13. Ephes. vi. 11—18. 2 St Pet. i. 5—11.

(*b*) 1 St John i. 7. (*c*) Ch. vii. 14, 23—25.

Person found himself thus intangled and overcome by Sin, I need not be much alarmed, if I often found myself in the same State.

P. It is greatly to be feared, *Eugenius*, that many others have made the same fatal Use of those Expressions; but I hope it will appear, that St *Paul* is not there speaking of *himself*; but of a very *different* Person.

And therefore let us hear him thus expostulating in the preceding Chapter. *Shall we continue in Sin, that Grace may abound? God forbid! How shall we that are dead to Sin, live any longer therein?—Knowing this, that our old Man is crucified with* Christ, *that the Body of Sin might be destroyed, that henceforth we should not serve Sin. For he that is dead, is freed from Sin. Now, if we be dead with* Christ, *we believe that we shall also live with him.* Ch. vi. 1, 2, 6, 7, 8.

Now, is it possible to conceive, that he who was thus *dead with Christ*, and *dead to Sin*; and therefore, according to his own Declaration, *freed from it*; is it possible to conceive, that this very Person was, at this very time, *sold under Sin,* that is, was neither *dead to it,* nor *freed from it?*

Again, let us observe how he addresses himself to the *Romans*, in this very Chapter.— *Likewise reckon ye also yourselves to be dead indeed unto Sin; but alive unto God, through* Jesus Christ *our Lord. Let not Sin therefore reign in your mortal Body, that you should obey it in the Lusts thereof. Neither yeild ye your Members,*

bers, as Instruments of Unrighteousness unto Sin: But yield yourselves unto God, as those that are alive from the Dead. — But now, being made free from Sin, and become Servants to God, ye have your Fruit unto Holiness, and the End everlasting Life. Ver. 11, 12, 13, 22.

Is it possible now for any *unprejudiced* Person to believe, that the inspired Apostle could thus talk to *others*; whilst *he himself* was *brought into Captivity to the Law of Sin?*

Again, he expresly assures those Converts, in these remarkable Words,—" The Law of " the Spirit of Life in *Christ Jesus,* hath made " me *free* from the *Law of Sin and Death.*" Ch. viii. 2.

But how was the Apostle made *free from the Law of Sin and Death*; whilst he was a *Slave* to the Law of *both?* Whilst he was *carnal, sold under Sin*; and under the *Terrors* of that *Death,* which is *the Wages of it?* Ch. vi. 23.—I know you have met with Writers, who have attempted to solve these Difficulties: But why will Men attempt to reconcile such *Absurdities* and *Contradictions?* Give me leave only to mention a Verse or two more out of this very Epistle. With how much Earnestness does this pious Man exhort those People to *present their Bodies a living Sacrifice, holy, acceptable unto God, which is,* says he, *your reasonable Service.* This, he *beseeches* them to do, *by the Mercies of God.* And moreover, that they would *not be conformed to this World*;
but

but that they would be *transformed by the renewing of their Mind*, Ch. xii. 1, 2.

Is not this *surprizing* Advice from a Person who had juſt been telling of them, that *he himſelf* was the *very reverſe* of this Character? He conjures *them* by the very *Mercies of God*, to preſent *their Bodies* a *living* and *holy Sacrifice*; whilſt he himſelf, *with his own Fleſh*, was actually *ſerving the Law of Sin!* Surely, if it was but a *reaſonable Service* for *them*, to preſent their *Bodies* an *holy Sacrifice to God*; it was full as *reaſonable* for their *Teacher* to do the ſame. But could he *preſent his Body a living Sacrifice, holy, and acceptable to God*; whilſt he was the *Servant* and *Slave of Sin?* Or could he follow the other Part of his Advice, to be *transformed by the renewing of the Mind*; and not to be *conformed to this World?*—For what is it to be *conformed to this World*; if the living in Sin be not? Or what is it to be *transformed by the renewing of the Mind*; but an entire Change of the Heart and Affections? And when they are thus changed, our outward Actions muſt certainly be changed too. We ſhall then *ſerve the Law of God*, both inwardly and outwardly. There will be no room to ſay,—*With the Mind I ſerve the Law of God; but with the Fleſh the Law of Sin.* Such a *Servant* of God, and *Servant of Sin*, is, in Truth and Reality, *no Servant of God* at all. For he that is *Truth* itſelf has aſſured us,— that *we cannot ſerve two* [ſuch] *Maſters*.—St. *Matt*. vi. 24.

But

But lastly, the same Apostle directs these Converts, — to *put on the Lord* Jesus Christ; *and not to make Provision for the Flesh*, to *fulfil the Lusts thereof*, chap. xiii. 14. From whence it seems evident, that he, who *with the Flesh serves the Law of Sin*, has not yet *put on the Lord Jesus*.—But shall we say, that this was the Case of the Apostle? That he had not *put on Christ*; though he admonished and exhorted those *Christians* to do it? Is not this to bring down an inspired Apostle to the level of those, *who profess to know God; but in Works deny him?* In short, this is so shocking an Opinion, that I could wish all that hold it would calmly and impartially reflect, whether, First, it does not make the holy Apostle flatly contradict himself in the same Breath? Secondly, whether those Converts, *being made free from Sin*, were not *much better Christians*, than he was himself? And, Thirdly, whether St *Paul* did not *give* much *better* Advice, than he had yet *taken?*

I do not by any means charge those with holding these Consequences, who maintain that Opinion: I only intreat such to divest themselves of all Prejudice, as far as possible, and attentively consider, whether that Opinion, and these Consequences, are not *inseparably* connected?

E. Indeed I think the State there described is much more suitable to such a carnal Wretch as I am, than to so holy and mortified a Person as St *Paul*.—But I now beg to know, what

what muſt be done, when we have forfeited the Benefit of our *Baptiſmal Regeneration?*

P. We muſt be recovered again, by the holy Spirit working in us *true Repentance,* and a *living Faith* in the *Blood of Chriſt* (a); and this Recovery of us by *Repentance* and *Faith* (which our Church in her *Catechiſm* enjoins to *all* who are *come to Age,* without Exception, may be well called a *Regeneration,* or *New Birth.*

E. I ſhould be glad to be informed, whether our Church calls any thing by the Name of *Regeneration,* or the *New Birth,* excepting *Baptiſm*; becauſe this is a Point which is ſometimes diſputed.

P. You will ſoon be able to judge of ſuch Diſputations: And therefore be pleaſed to obſerve, in the firſt Place, that in the *Homily* for *Whitſunday,* after mention is made of the Power of the *Holy Ghoſt,* in altering and changing of Mankind, and making us *New Men* in *Chriſt Jeſus,* it thus follows,——
" Such is the Power of the *Holy Ghoſt* to *re-*
" *generate Men,* and, as it were, to *bring*
" *them forth a-new,* ſo that they ſhall be no-
" thing like the Men that they were before.
" Neither doth [the Holy Spirit] think it
" ſufficient inwardly to work the ſpiritual and
" *New-Birth* of Man, unleſs he do alſo *dwell*
" and *abide* in him."

And

(a) St Luke xxiv. 47.   Acts viii. 22, 23.   Chap. xx. 21.   Rom. iii. 25.   Chap. v. 1.   Ephes. ii. 8. 2 Tim. ii. 25, 26.

And at the Conclusion, we have the following Words, ——— "Humbly beseeching [God] so to work in our Hearts, by the Power of his holy Spirit, that we being *regenerate*, and *newly born again* in all Goodness, Righteousness, Sobriety, and Truth, may, in the end, be made Partakers of everlasting Life in his heavenly Kingdom (*a*)."—Moreover, what is it to be *raised from the Death of Sin unto the Life of Righteousness* (*b*)? — What is it to be *new-created* from a wicked Person to a *righteous* Man; which our Church mentions from St *Austin* (*c*)? What is it so truly to repent, as to be clean *altered and changed*; and to become *New Creatures*; and to walk in a *New Life* as *New-born-Babes* (*d*)?

What is it to be *daily renewed* by the Holy Spirit (*e*)? What is it to have *New Hearts created* in us (*f*)? What do all these various Expressions mean, but the very same Thing with being *regenerate* and *newly born again?*

Moreover, what else does the Holy Ghost design by that *New Heart* and *New Spirit*, which are promised to true Penitents (*g*)?

What

(*a*) Hom. for *Whitsunday*, Part i. p. 276, 278. Edit. *London*, 1726.
(*b*) Last Collect in the Funeral Office.
(*c*) Hom. for *Rogation-week*, Part i. p. 286.
(*d*) Hom. of Repentance, Part ii. p. 327, 328.
(*e*) Collect for *Christmas-day*.
(*f*) Collect for *Ash-wednesday*.
(*g*) Ezek. xi. 19. Ch. xviii. 31. Ch. xxxvi. 26.

What else does our Holy Lord mean by this Saying,—" Except ye be *converted*, and " *become* as *little Children*, ye shall not enter " into the Kingdom of Heaven (*a*)?" What else does St *Paul* mean by the being *transformed by the renewing of the Mind* (*b*)? What else is to be understood by *mortifying the Deeds of the Body through the Spirit:* And by *crucifying the Flesh, with the Affections and Lusts* (*c*)? What is it to *set the Affections on Things above; to put off the old Man; to be renewed in the Spirit of the Mind; and to put on the new Man, which, after God, is created in Righteousness and true Holiness* (*d*)? What does the same Apostle mean in two Places, by a *New Creature* (*e*); but only such a Person as St *Chrysostom* describes in the following Manner? *He is turned into a New Creature: For he is born again* [*or from above*] *through the Spirit* (*f*). But still further; What can St *Peter* design by these following Words,— " *being born again—of incorruptible Seed, by* " *the Word of God, which liveth and abideth* " *for ever* (*g*)? Or what does St *John* mean, when he declares, that " *Whosoever is born of* " *God, doth not commit Sin;*—that *Whatsoever* " *is born of God, overcometh the World;*—And that

---

(*a*) St Matth. xviii. 3.   (*b*) Rom. xii. 2.
(*c*) Rom. viii. 13. Gal. v. 24.
(*d*) Ephes. iv. 22—24. Colos. iii. 1, 2, 9, 10.
(*e*) 2 Cor. v. 11. Gal. vi. 15.
(*f*) Εἰς ἑτέραν ἦλθε δημιουργίαν, κ̀ γὰρ ἄνωθεν ἐγεννήθη διὰ πνεύματ⟨Θ⟩. in 2 Cor. v. 11. Edit. *Commel.* 1603. p. 819. M.   (*g*) 1 Epist. i. 23.

that "*Whosoever is born of God, sinneth not;
but he that is begotten of God, keepeth himself; and that wicked One toucheth him
not* (a) ?" —— So that not only our own
Church, but what is of infinitely greater Authority, the Divine Oracles, seem plainly to
call this entire Change of the whole Man, by
the Name of *Regeneration* (b), or *New-Birth*.
I omit those other Passages in the sacred Writings, where our Blessed Lord speaks of the
being *born again*; *born of Water, and of the
Spirit* (c): and where St *Paul* mentions our
*being saved by the washing of Regeneration, and
renewing of the Holy Ghost* (d); because they
immediately relate to the miraculous Effects
of the Holy Spirit in *Baptism*. However,
with regard to the *new creating a Sinner from
a wicked Person to a righteous Man*, which
St *Austin* affirms to be *a greater Miracle than
to make a new Heaven and Earth* (e); I say,
with regard to this, whoever is thus *altered*
and *changed*, and, as it were, *new created* by
the Spirit of God, though many Years *after*
his *Baptism*, is surely as much *born of the
Spirit*, as the Person who is *regenerated* at
the time he is *baptized*. It is evidently *one*
and the *same Spirit*, that works; and indeed
the *same Work* of *that Spirit*; only manifest-
ing

(a) 1 Epist. iii. 9. Ch. v. 4, 18.
(b) Ἀναγεννήσας ἡμᾶς —— Having *begotten us again,*
1 St Pet. i. 3. —— ἀναγεγεννημένοι, *being born again,*
Chap. i. 23.
(c) St John iii. 3, 5.   (d) Titus iii. 5.
(e) Hom. for *Rogation-week*, Part i. P. 286.

ing his divine Power at different Seasons. For instead of being *a Child of Wrath*, the Sinner is become *a Child of Grace*; *a Member of Christ*; *a Child of God*; *and an Inheritor of the Kingdom of Heaven*. He is to be henceforth *dead unto Sin, and alive unto God*; and to *put on the new Man, which, after God, is created in Righteousness and true Holiness*. And therefore, both from the Nature of the Thing, as well as from the Nature of the Expressions used in the *sacred Writings*, such a *thorough and entire Change of the Heart and Affections*, wrought by the Holy Spirit of God, may, with the greatest Propriety, be called a *Regeneration* or *New Birth*. The two famous Fathers, just mentioned, do, in effect, give it this Name (*a*). Our Church, you see, expressly calls it so; and she has manifestly abundant Reason for so doing; since such a *Renewal of the whole Man*, is the being *born again*,— at what Time or Season, or under what Circumstances soever, this *spiritual Birth* may happen.

E. As I find they are evidently mistaken, who suppose our Church calls nothing by the Name of a *Regeneration* or *New Birth*, but only *Baptism*: So, what is of the highest Concern to me, I find very plainly the Need I have of being thus *regenerated* or *born again* by the Holy Spirit.

P. Be

(*a*) See also St *Chrysostom* on *Gal.* iv. 19. Page 1010, where we meet with this in express Words, ἀναγεννήσεως ἑτέρας ὑμῖν δεῖ, καὶ ἀναπλάσεως —*You want another Regeneration, and to be formed anew*.

P. Be thankful, my dear Friend, that the Holy Spirit has begun this great Work in you: For the first Step in order to a *spiritual New Birth*, is to be thoroughly *convinced* of the Danger we are in from Sin. The Holy Spirit must work this *Conviction* (*a*) in us; and excite some Desires in our Hearts of being *delivered from the Wrath to come* (*b*). So that this is a very happy Beginning; but the Misfortune of too many is, they either see not their Danger, or, when they do, yet they like not this *uneasy State*; and therefore are apt to fly from it, and consequently, from their own Salvation. However, I am persuaded, that this will never be your Case.

E. I hope in God, it never will: And therefore desire to know, what is to be done upon such *Conviction?*

P. Fly immediately to *Christ*; who has invited *all heavy-laden Sinners to come to him*; and has promised to *give them rest* (*c*).

E. But does not our holy Lord say,—*No man can come to me, except the Father, which hath sent me, draw him* (*d*)? How then can I go to *Christ?*

P. Remember, my dear *Eugenius*, that when the Holy Spirit has any way opened your Mind, by any Means or Method whatever, and thus convinced you of your State, and has touched your Heart to fly to a *Saviour*,

(*a*) St John xvi. 8. Acts xxvi. 18.
(*b*) Ch. ii. 37. Ch. ix. 6. Ch. xvi. 29, 30. 1 Thess. i. 10. St Matth. iii. 7.
(*c*) St Matth. xi. 28.   (*d*) St John vi. 44.

viour, God then *draws you to Christ*; and you must immediately run to him.

And further, it is our Duty often to implore, that God would *lighten our Darkness*; and to pray with pious *Elihu*,—That which *I see not teach thou me* (*a*).

Our blessed Saviour assures us, that *he stands at the Door and knocks* (*b*): But the great Misfortune of Mankind is, that they turn a deaf Ear to him; though he thus graciously and frequently admonishes every one, —*he that hath Ears to hear, let him hear* (*c*). As if our holy Lord had said,—*Let each carefully attend to my Voice*; *that I may no longer call in vain*.

And moreover, all should remember, that God is perpetually calling every Sinner to Repentance by his divine Gospel (*d*); and therefore every Sinner has a constant Call to fly to *Christ*. And indeed *to whom* else *shall we go?* For *he* only *has the Words of eternal Life* (*e*): *he is the Way, and the Truth, and the Life*: and *no Man cometh unto the Father, but by him* (*f*). — Let therefore every Sinner fly to him, without delay; for he, and he only, is their *City of Refuge*.

E. You give me great Encouragement to go to *Christ*; but my manifold Sins and Corruptions are enough to deter me.

P. Know

(*a*) Job xxxiv. 32.   (*b*) Rev. iii. 20.
(*c*) St Matth. xi. 15.
(*d*) St Mark i. 15.   St Luke xxiv. 47.   Acts ii. 38. Ch. xvii. 30. Rom. ii. 4. Ephes. v. 14.
(*e*) St John vi. 68.   (*f*) Ch. xiv. 6.

P. Know you not, that the Lord *Jesus* came not to call the Righteous, *but Sinners to Repentance:* and that *the Whole need not a Physician, but they that are Sick* (a)? The *self-righteous,* and such as are *whole* in their own Eyes, see but little Want of the great Physician of Souls; very little Want of a *Saviour.* They may often hear his gracious Voice; but not perceiving the miserable State they are in; (their own *Self-righteousness* having blinded their Eyes) they can only approach *Christ* in a mere *formal* manner; but *feel* not that they are lost and undone *without* him.

These are the very Persons whom our holy Lord thus describes, —— *Thou sayest I am rich, and increased with Goods, and have need of nothing; and knowest not that thou art wretched, and miserable, and poor, and blind, and naked* (b).

Let not then the *Sight* of your *Corruptions* keep you from *Christ,* but rather persuade you immediately to fly to him. However, be careful to approach him, like a *true returning, contrite* Sinner; like one, who sees his Danger, and is desirous to avoid it.——
Therefore thus confess every Sin of your Soul. Humbly beseech the Lord *Jesus* that you may be *washed from your Sins in his Blood* (c); and that you may have the full Benefit of *that Fountain* which is *opened for Sin and for Uncleanness* (d). That you may be

(a) St Luke v. 31, 32.   (b) Rev. iii. 17.
(c) Rev. i. 5.   (d) Zechar. xiii. 1.

be cleansed from that *Corruption* of your *Nature*, that *polluted Heart*; from whence have proceeded every *evil Thought*, and every *evil Work* (a). That you may be delivered from *that Law which wars against the Law of your Mind, and brings you into Captivity to the Law of Sin.* That you may be delivered from *that carnal Mind,* which is *Enmity against God: For it is not subject to the Law of God, neither indeed can be* (b). Pray that *the Law of the Spirit of Life in Christ Jesus, may make you free from the Law of Sin and Death* (c).

Sincerely labour to *bring forth Fruits meet for Repentance* (d); to avoid all Sin, and every Occasion of it; and, to the best of your Abilities, to obey every Precept of the Gospel. —— Strive to undo every thing you have done amiss: And, to the utmost of your Power, make *Restitution* (e). Petition for that true *godly Sorrow*, which worketh *Repentance to Salvation*; pray earnestly and constantly that the Holy Spirit may always assist you; may open your Mind and influence your Heart; and carry you through the whole Work: And that he may compleat in you *Repentance towards God*; and *Faith towards our Lord Jesus Christ* (f).

Them, who thus come unto *Christ*; or, which is the same thing, them, who thus

come

(a) Psalm li. 5. St Matth. xv. 18, 19.
(b) Rom. vii. 23, 24. Ch. viii. 7.
(c) Rom. viii. 2.   (d) St Matth. iii. 8.
(e) Job xx. 18. Ezek. xxxiii. 15. St Luke xix. 8, 9.
(f) Acts xx. 21. Philip. i. 6.

come unto God *by him, he is able* [and ready] *to save to the uttermost: Seeing he ever liveth to make Intercession for them* (*a*).

E. I pray God grant I may be of that Number: But I beg to know, in how many Respects *Christ* is a *Saviour* to us?

P. Christ saves us from the *Power of Satan* (*b*). He saves us from the *Guilt* of Sin, and the *Punishment* (*c*) due to it. He likewise saves us from the *Dominion* of it; from its *reigning* and *condemning* Power (*d*) --- He is a *Saviour*, and *mighty to save* (*e*), in all these respects: But if we refuse him in *one*, we refuse him in *all*. He will save none *in* their Sins: For he came on purpose to save us *from* them (*f*). *God sent him to bless us, in turning away every one of us from his Iniquities* (*g*).

The great Design of *Christ* was *to make an end of Sin; and to bring in everlasting Righteousness* (*h*). Therefore whoever will not be *turned from his Iniquities*, he opposes the great Designs of *Christ*. He is for keeping *out* everlasting Righteousness; by not suffering *Sin to be made an end of*. For how is *Sin to be made an end of*, whilst he continues it both in his Heart and Practice? Or how is *everlasting Righte-*

(*a*) Heb. vii. 25.
(*b*) Acts xxvi. 18. Colos. i. 13. Heb. ii. 14, 15.
(*c*) Ephes. i. 7. Rev. i. 5. Rom. v. 9. 1 Thess. i. 10.
(*d*) Rom. vi. 6, 7, 11—15, 18, 22. ch. viii. 2—4. 1 Cor. xv. 56, 57.
(*e*) Isaiah lxiii. 1. (*f*) St Matth. i. 21.
(*g*) Acts iii. 26. (*h*) Daniel ix. 24.

Righteousness to be brought in, whilst he keeps it *out* of his Heart and Actions (*a*)?

If a Man should fancy he might still be *blest* with this *everlasting Righteousness*, though he persisted in his Sins and Wickedness, let him hearken to the Words of the holy Spirit just mentioned,—God sent [Christ] to *bless* us, in *turning away* every one of us *from* his Iniquities. Consequently that Man *cannot* be *blest* by *Christ*; he cannot have a share in the *Blessing* of *Christ*'s *everlasting Righteousness*, who will *not* be *turned from* his Sins. Nothing is more evident to a Man, who can but open his Eyes.

E. To me, I must own, the Matter appears perfectly plain: And therefore may I be truly and effectually *turned* from *all* mine. But now, since there must be *Faith* as well as *Repentance*, I desire to know, whether they must be united; or whether one is to come before the other?

P. You are to observe, that as *Repentance and Remission of Sins are to be preached in the Name of Christ*; and it being *through him only that we are reconciled to God* (*b*); it is impossible either to go to *Christ*, or to God thro' *him*, or in his *Name*, without at least some *general Belief* that *Christ* is *the Propitiation for the Sins of the World*.

E. But

(*a*) This was the Paragraph referred to, P. 7, Note c.
(*b*) St Luke xxiv. 47. Acts xiii. 32. 2 Cor. v. 18, 19. Ephes. ii. 13—18.

E. But is *this* the *Faith*, by which we are said to be *justified?*

P. It is not: You will find *justifying Faith* to be a different thing.

E. Pray, what is meant by *Justification?*

P. The *Remission or Forgiveness* of Sins (*a*).

E. But how am I to understand these Sayings of St *Paul*, that *a Man is justified by Faith, without the Deeds of the Law* (*b*): And that *by the Works of the Law, shall no Flesh be justified* (*c*)?

P. Saint *Paul* evidently designs to affirm, that neither the Law of *Nature*, nor the Law of *Moses* could *justify Sinners.* For as *all Mankind*

(*a*) It is certain that *Justification* is properly a *forensic* Term; and taken in its full Extent, is of a very comprehensive Meaning. It implies a *judicial* Sentence, by which the Sinner is *absolved* from *Guilt*, and consequently *discharged* from *Punishment*.

And moreover, through the same *Faith*, by which we are thus *justified*, we become the *Sons of God*, and receive a *Title* to the *Heavenly Inheritance* *. St *John* i. 12, 13. *Gal.* iii. 24, 26. Ch. iv. 6, 7. *Rom.* viii. 17. *Ephes.* ii. 4.

However, as the *Remission* or *Forgiveness of Sins* necessarily implies a *Discharge* both from *Guilt* and *Punishment*, and can only be embraced by that *Divine Faith*, which gives a *Title* to our being *Sons of God*, and *Heirs* of his Kingdom; therefore *Justification* may be very well explained, in general, by the *Forgiveness* or *Remission of Sins.* — And indeed the *Apostle* himself seems plainly to describe it under this general Notion.—— See *Rom.* iii. 24—26. Ch. iv. 5—8. *Homily of Salvation*, Part I. Page 11.

(*b*) Rom. iii. 28.   (*c*) Gal. ii. 16.

* See the learned *Gataker* on *Isaiab* v. 23. Ch. liii. 11. And the late Reverend and Pious Dr *Doddridge* on Acts. iii. 20, Note *a*; where he also quotes the learned *Vitringa.*

kind were become guilty before God (*a*), and stood condemned by the one Law, or by the other; it was impossible for them to be acquitted by either. But God of his *free Grace* engaged to *justify* or pardon a sinful World, upon a *living Faith* in the *Blood* of his Son (*b*). However, this *Faith* was to be preceded by *unfeigned Repentance* (*c*): And to discover its Truth and Reality, as Opportunity offered, by *sincere* and *universal Obedience* (*d*).

But still, we are not to imagine that our *Faith* has any more *Merit* than our *Works*. Our *Justification* or *Pardon* proceeds entirely from the *free Grace* of God in *Christ*: And it is embraced, or applied to the Soul by *such a Faith*, as the Holy Spirit must work in us (*e*).

Hence

(*a*) Rom. iii. 9, 19, 20, 23.
(*b*) Ch. iii. 21, 22, 24, 25. Gal. ii. 16. Ch. iii. 26. Ch. v. 6   Ephes. i. 7.   Ch. ii. 5, 8.
(*c*) Acts ii. 38. Ch. xx. 21. Ch xxvi 18, 20.
(*d*) St Matth. vii 21. St John xiv. 15, 21, 23, 24. Ch. xv. 14, 16. Col i. 10. Heb xiii 21. 1 St Pet. i. 2. 2 Epist. i 5—8.   1 St John ii. 3—5.   Ch. iii. 3—10.
(*e*) St Mark ix. 24.   St Luke xvii 5.   St John i 12, 13.   2 Cor. iv. 13.   Gal. v. 22.   Ephes ii 8.   Philip. i 29.   Ch. ii. 13.   2 Thess. i 11.   2 Peter i. 1. " *Faith*, says a very learned and worthy *Prelate*, " *which is the* " *Principle of the Gospel, respects the Promises and Decla-* " *rations of God, and includes a sure Trust and Reliance on* " *him for the Performance:* " Bp *Sherlock*'s *Discourses*, the *last Disc.* and *Part* 1. But I must beg leave here to add, that *this Faith* is not the Product of *Reading, Study,* or *Reflection*; but the pure genuine Work of the *Spirit* of *Christ*. This appears from most of the Texts above referred to: And indeed thus much may sufficiently be concluded, from the very Nature of it. For since it is a

Principle

Hence it is, that we are sometimes said to be *justified by God*, or *by his Grace*; sometimes by the *Blood of Christ*, or the *Redemption* which is in *him*; and sometimes by *Faith* (*a*).

The *free Grace*, or *Goodness* of God, may be called the *First*, or *Principal or Efficient* Cause of our *Justification*; the *Blood of Christ*, or in other Words, *what Christ has done and suffered*, is the *meritorious* Cause of it; and *that Faith*, by which we embrace our *Pardon* or *Justification*, may be esteemed, as it were, the *Instrument* (*b*) of it. And when the Holy Spirit has wrought this *Faith* in a *mourning* Sinner, how welcome to the Soul must be that joyful Voice! —*Son, be of good cheer, thy Sins be forgiven thee* (*c*). For *being justified by Faith*,

Principle by which the *Heart is purified*, and which discovers itself by [a divine] *Love* to God and Man [Acts xv. 9. Ch. xxvi. 18. Gal. v. 6.] it must demonstrate its Origin to be from Heaven. As it is evidently a Part of our *new Creation*, it must be like every other Part, the *Work of God*; and thus it is called in express Terms,— *Faith of the Operation of God*, Colos. ii. 12.——*Faith*, τῆς ἐνεργείας τοῦ Θεοῦ,—*Faith*, wrought by the *Energy*, or *efficacious Power of God*: And therefore it is no wonder it should make so considerable a Part of the *Armour of God*, Ephes. vi. 13, 14, 16, compared with 1 Thess. v. 8.— However, though it be not a *Faith of our own working*; it is a *Faith* that may be procured by our own *honest* and *earnest Diligence*. Seek it by *humble and constant Prayer*, and thou shalt find it. — Therefore, if thou hast it not, lay the Fault on thyself only.

(*a*) Rom. iii. 24, 25. Ch. v. 1, 9. Ch. viii. 33. Tit. iii. 7.

(*b*) Hom. of the Passion, Part II. p. 258, 259.

(*c*) St Matth. ix. 2.

Faith, we have PEACE with God, through our Lord Jesus Christ (a).—*He is our Peace* (b); having made Peace, through the Blood of his Cross (c). He is our *Propitiation*, or *Mercy-seat* (d), *through Faith in his Blood*. To such as approach this *Mercy seat* by a *living Faith*, God discovers himself a reconciled Father (e). At that instant, his divine Kingdom begins to be set up in the Soul: And where this Kingdom is, *Peace* will discover itself. *For the Kingdom of God is Righteousness, and Peace, and Joy in the Holy Ghost* (f).—Consequently, *Peace with God* appears to be the certain Result of *justifying Faith*: And our Church's Notion of such a Faith seems perfectly right.
—" This, she says, *is given us of God*; and
" is a *sure Trust and Confidence* in God, that
" by the Merits of *Christ* [a Man's] Sins *be*
" *forgiven* and he *reconciled* to the Favour of
" God, and to *be Partaker* of the Kingdom of
" Heaven by *Christ* (g)." Again, " *Faith* is
" said to be a *sure Trust and Confidence* in the
" Mercies of God: whereby we *persuade* our-
" selves, that God both *hath*, and *will* for-
" give *our* Sins; that he *hath* accepted *us*
" again into his Favour; that he *hath* releas-
" ed *us* from the Bonds of Damnation," &c.
" We must *apprehend* the Merits of *Christ*'s
         " Death

(a) **Rom.** v. 1.   (b) Ephes. ii. 14.
(c) Colos. i. 20.   (d) 'Ιλαστήριον. Rom. iii. 25.
(e) Ch. v. 8—11. 2 Cor. v. 18, 19. Ephes. ii. 16—18.
1 Tim. ii. 5, 6. Heb. vii. 25. Ch. x. 19—22.
(f) Rom. xiv. 17.
(g) Hom. of Salvation, Part III. p. 16, 17.

"Death and Passion—with a *strong* and *stedfast Faith, nothing doubting* but that *Christ* —*hath* taken away *Our* Sins, and *hath* restored *us* again into God's Favour (a)." Elsewhere we meet with what follows,— "*Thou hast* received [our Saviour Jesus Christ] if in *true Faith* and *Repentance* of Heart thou hast received him.—*Thou hast received* his Body, to endow *thee* with everlasting Righteousness, to *assure thee* of the everlasting Bliss and Life of thy Soul. For with *Christ*, by *true Faith*, art *thou* quickened again,—from Death of Sin, to Life of Grace (b)." And only to mention one Place more,—" A *sure* and *constant Faith*, not only that the Death of *Christ* is available for the Redemption of *all the World*, for the Remission of Sins, and Reconciliation with God the Father; but also that he hath made, upon his Cross, a full and sufficient Sacrifice for *thee*, a perfect cleansing of *thy* Sins;—and that thou mayest say with the Apostle, that he loved *thee*, and gave himself for *thee* (c)."

So that *justifying Faith*, according to our Church, and, I presume, according to the Apostle, is such a Faith wrought by the Holy Spirit, as causes a Man *firmly* to *believe* that *his* Sins are actually forgiven; that *God in Christ* is reconciled to him, and that *Christ* is become

---

(a) Hom. of the Passion, Part II. p. 258.
(b) Hom. of the Resurrection, p. 262.
(c) Hom. of the Sacrament, Part I. p. 269.

become *a Propitiation* for *his* Sins in particular. These are the Sentiments of our Church; and they appear to be excellently founded. And where is the Wonder, if from hence should arise great Comfort and Satisfaction to the Mind: Since *being thus justified by Faith*, a Man must *have Peace with God, through our Lord* Jesus Christ? But now *this Faith is the Operation of God* (*a*), or of his Holy Spirit, as has been already observed; and it will be wrought in every sincere Penitent, when infinite Wisdom shall judge it proper. And as such a *Faith* is the *Substance* or Foundation *of Things hoped for*; and the *Evidence*, or Conviction, *of Things not seen* (*b*): As such a *Faith* will, in time, *purify the Heart* (*c*) entirely; will *quench all the fiery Darts of the Wicked* (*d*); and give us the *Victory over this World* (*e*); is it at all to be wondered at, that so divine a Principle should enable us to embrace the *Promises of God in Christ*; and that our *Justification* should be ascribed to it, in the manner we have explained?

Our Church may certainly, with the highest Reason, declare, that the being *justified by Faith only, is a most wholesome Doctrine, and very full of Comfort* (*f*).

For

(*a*) Colos. ii. 12. Hom. of Salvation, Part I. p. 13. Part III. p. 16.
  (*b*) Heb. xi. 1.   (*c*) Acts xv. 9.
  (*d*) Ephes. vi. 16.   (*e*) 1 St John v. 4.
  (*f*) Article XI.

For if it be the *Doctrine* of the *holy Spirit*, as is manifestly evident, it must surely be a *most wholesome Doctrine:* And if *the Peace of God* be the certain Consequence of being *justified by Faith*, as the Spirit of Truth affirms, it is manifestly *a Doctrine full of Comfort*. And withal, since the Spirit of God has so often mentioned (*a*) it, I must take leave to think, that it is a *Doctrine* of *no small* Importance.

E. Is it then possible for a Person ever to *know* when his Sins are pardoned? For this I have observed to be often questioned.

P. There is nothing, *Eugenius*, which Men may *not* question, when they are so disposed. But I believe you will think there is little Reason to make any Doubt of this, when you have considered it a little further.—Pray attend to the Words of our holy Lord,—*Come unto me, all ye that labour, and are heavy laden, and I will give you Rest* (*b*).

But now, is it possible for the *labouring*, and *heavy laden* Sinner to *have Rest*; and yet *not* to *know* it? Can a wounded Conscience be *healed*; and the Man *not* be *sensible* of it? Can God speak *Joy* and *Peace* to the Soul (*c*); and yet that Soul be a Stranger to *Joy* and *Peace?* Is not a guilty *awakened* Conscience

like

(*a*) Acts xiii. 38, 39. Rom. iii. 22, 25, 26, 28, 30. Ch. iv. 5. Ch. v. 1. Ch. ix. 30—32. Gal. ii. 16. Ch. iii. 11, 14, 22, 24, 26. Ch. v. 5, 6 Ephes. ii. 8. Philip. iii. 9. (*b*) St Matth. xi. 28.
(*c*) Rom xv. 13.

like the troubled Sea, when it cannot reſt? There is *no Peace, faith my God, to the Wicked* (*a*). Such a State is a Hell upon Earth; there is nothing but *Tumult*, and *Horror*, and *Deſpair*. But when once ſuch a Conſcience is *waſhed by the Blood of Chriſt* (*b*), there is a *Calm*, and *Peace*, and *Comfort*.

And cannot the Man, do you think, eaſily find a *Difference* between the two States? It may as well be queſtioned, whether a Man knows the Difference between being upon a *Rack*, and lying *at Eaſe* in his Bed: This *ſpiritual Diſcernment* our Church ſpeaks of in more Places than one.

"If after Contrition, ſays our Church, we "*feel* our Conſciences at *Peace with God*, "through Remiſſion of our Sin, and to be "reconciled again to his Favour;—Who "worketh theſe great Miracles in us?—God "give us Grace to *know* theſe Things, and "to *feel* them in our Hearts (*c*)." Again, ſpeaking of the bleſſed *Sacrament*, ſhe uſes this Expreſſion,—— "Here [the Faithful] "may *feel* wrought the *Tranquillity* of Con- "ſcience, (*d*) &c." And in another Homily, ſpeaking of *a true lively Faith*, we have theſe Words,—"If you *feel* and per- "ceive ſuch a *Faith* in you, rejoice in it (*e*)." And in the *Viſitation Office*, this is one of the
Petitions,

(*a*) Iſaiah v. 7, 20, 21.
(*b*) Heb. ix. 14. Coloſ. i. 20. 1 St John i. 7. Rev. i 5.
(*c*) Hom. for Rogation-week, Part. III. p. 292, 293.
(*d*) Hom. of the Sacrament, Part I. p. 269.
(*e*) Hom. on Faith, Part III. p. 26.

Petitions,—" Make thee *know* and *feel* that there is none other Name—in whom, and thro' whom, thou mayeſt receive Health and Salvation." And in the ſame Office, in the Prayer for *Perſons troubled* in *Mind or* in *Conſcience*, theſe are part of the Petitions,—" Make him to *hear* of Joy and Gladneſs, that the Bones which thou haſt broken may *rejoice.* Deliver him from *fear* of the Enemy, and lift up the *Light of thy Countenance* upon him, and give him *Peace, &c."* What is this *hearing* of Joy and Gladneſs, and this *rejoicing* of *broken Bones*, but a ſpiritual *Diſcernment* of Comfort in that Conſcience, which was before *broken* and *wounded* by a Senſe of Guilt? Or what is this *Deliverance* from *fear* of the *Enemy*; and the *lifting up the Light of God's Countenance*, and *giving Peace*, but freeing a troubled Soul from the Darkneſs and Horrors of Deſpair; and from the *fiery Darts* of the Devil, which a *Chriſtian* is to *quench* by the *Shield of Faith* (*a*): And to cauſe that dark and troubled Soul *to ſee* that *Light of Life*, and to *feel* that *Peace of God, which paſſeth all Underſtanding* (*b*)? And moreover, what does our Church mean by this Petition at the Concluſion of the *Litany*,—*O Lamb of God, that takeſt away the Sins of the World, grant us thy Peace?* What can ſhe mean by the *Calm* of *Conſcience*, which muſt always ariſe from a *Senſe* of the pardon-

ing

(*a*) Epheſ. vi. 16.
(*b*) St John viii. 12. Philip. iv. 7.

ing Love of God?' Pray, observe how she represents the Agonies of a *real* Penitent; — *Pitifully behold the Sorrows of our Hearts. The Remembrance of* [our Sins] *is grievous unto us: The Burden of them is intolerable. Receive and comfort us, who are grieved and wearied with the Burden of our Sins* (a).

Undoubtedly such as speak these Things from the *Heart*, must always be thoroughly *sensible* when these *piercing Sorrows*, when these *grievous and intolerable Burdens* are removed. Though, indeed, as for those who repeat these Sentences only by *rote*; who *feel no Burden*, who experience *no Sorrows* of Heart; how is it possible they should perceive the *Removal* of that, which they never once *felt?* But then as this Load is not like to be removed, till Men do really *feel* it; may the Holy Spirit effectually work in them a *spiritual Discernment*, that they may no longer trifle with God and their own Salvation.

E. I am fully satisfied, both from the Nature of the Thing, and from the Sentiments of our own Church, that Men may very *sensibly perceive* when God has absolved them from their *Guilt.*—God grant I may one Day, through the Merits of *Christ*, have the same blessed Experience!

P. I doubt not, my dear Friend, but you will. However, this ought carefully to be remembered,

---

(a) See the latter End of the Litany; the general Confession in the Communion-Office; and the Commination-Service.

remembered, that every *justified* Person must not immediately look for a *perpetual Calm*; or to be always free from *many*, and perhaps *severe Temptations:* But still he will *find Grace to help in time of Need* (*a*). He is no longer the *Servant of Sin* (*b*). Nor *will God suffer him to be tempted above that he is able*; *but will with the Temptation also make a Way to escape, that he may be able to bear it* (*c*). However, if there should be, for some time, a Succession of *Light* and *Gloominess*, of *Hope* and *Doubting*; these should not disquiet a *Christian*; or cause him to mistrust the Safety of his Condition. But he ought constantly to persevere in humble Prayer, with Patience and Submission: And God's Holy Spirit will carry him on *from Strength to Strength*; and from one Degree of *Faith* and *Holiness* to another (*d*).

E. But how may this *true justifying Faith* be distinguished from that which is *false* and *counterfeit*; which St *James* says is dead, and which cannot *save* or *justify* (*e*)?

P. They may very easily be distinguished, with a little Care and Attention. *True justifying Faith* not only brings Peace to the Mind, but is a living Principle of *Universal Obedience*; discovering itself by an *unfeigned Love to God and*

(*a*) Heb. iv. 16.   (*b*) Rom. vi. 6.
(*c*) 1 Cor. x. 13.
(*d*) Psalm lxxxiv. 7.   St John i. 16.   Rom. i. 17. Ephes. iv. 13.   Philip. i. 6.
(*e*) St James ii. 14, 17, 20, 22, 24, 26.

and Man. Inclining us to walk in *every* Command of *Chrift*; and to endeavour to *bring forth much Fruit*; and even to be *filled with the Fruits of Righteoufnefs* (a). This is that *Breaft-plate of Righteoufnefs,* or of *Faith* and *Love,* which *Chriftians* are directed to *arm* themfelves with (b). — Whereas the *Faith* which is condemned by St *James,* is a *Faith deftitute* of the Love of God and Man: A *Faith* which brings not forth *the Fruits of the Gofpel:* But is *barren* and *dead;* and therefore *vain,* and void of all *Efficacy.* — Such a *Faith* as *this* is confiftent with cherifhing *Anger, Malice, Pride, Covetoufnefs,* or any other corrupt Difpofition whatever. Nay it is confiftent with every *evil Word,* and every *vicious Action.* But where *true Faith is,* it both *juftifies* and will *fanctify* (c); nor does it give any Indulgence to fuch *Works of the Devil.* The Holy Spirit declares, that *he that committeth Sin, is of the Devil* (d). *Whofoever abideth in* [Chrift] *finneth not. Whofoever is born of God, doth not commit Sin:* And moreover, that *in this the Children of God are manifeft, and the Children of the Devil: Whofoever doth not Righteoufnefs, is not of God* (e). Confequently, *that Faith,* which does not begin to *purify the Heart,*

fpeaks

(a) St Matth. 22. 37—40. St John xiii. 34, 35. Ch. xv 2, 4, 5, 8, 10. Gal. v. 6. Philip. i. 11. 1St John iii. 15—19, 22—24. Ch. iv. 16—21.
(b) Ephes. vi. 14. 1 Thefs. v. 8.
(c) Acts xxvi. 18. 1 Cor. vi. 11.
(d) 1 St John iii. 8.   (e) Ver. 6, 9, 10.

speaks only a *deceitful* Peace to us (*a*). The *Blood of Chrift*, when rightly applied, always brings *Peace* (*b*); but then it will always *purge the Confcience from dead Works to serve the living God* (*c*).

His *precious Blood* is a *fanctifying* Principle (*d*); it *redeems from a vain*, and wicked *Converfation* (*e*); it *turns* them, who are *fanctified by Faith in Chrift, from the Power of Satan* (*f*); and confequently, from the *Works of Satan*: For *Chrift was manifefted to deftroy the Works of the Devil* (*g*). They that are *Elect*, are *Elect——through Sanctification of the Spirit unto Obedience, and fprinkling of the Blood of* Jefus Chrift (*h*).——*Seeing*, fays the fame Apoftle, *ye have purified your Souls in obeying the Truth through the Spirit* (*i*).

You fee, my dear *Eugenius*, how *true Faith* in the *Blood of Chrift*; *Sanctification* of *Heart* and *Life*; and *unfeigned Obedience*, muft and ever will, have a mutual Connection with one another. But let us ftill attend to the Doctrine of the Holy Spirit a little further. —" The Grace of God that bringeth Sal-
" vation, hath appeared to all Men; teach-
" ing us, that, denying Ungodlinefs and
" worldly Lufts, we fhould live *foberly, righ-*
" *teoufly*, and *godly* in this prefent World;
" looking

(*a*) Acts xv. 9.
(*b*) Rom. xiv. 17.   Ephes. ii. 13, 14.   Col. i. 20.
(*c*) Heb. ix. 14.   (*d*) Heb. xiii. 12.
(*e*) 1 St Peter i. 8, 19.   (*f*) Acts xxvi. 18.
(*g*) 1 St John iii. 8.   (*h*) 1 St Peter i. 2.
(*i*) Ch. i. 22.

"looking for that blessed Hope, and the
"glorious appearing of the great God, and
"our Saviour *Jesus Christ:* Who gave him-
"self for us, that he might *redeem* us from
"*all Iniquity,* and *purify* unto himself a *pe-*
"*culiar* People *zealous of good Works* (a)."—
I desire you would consider, whether those who are *not* zealous of *good Works*, can be of the Number of this *peculiar People?*

Again, the same Holy Spirit, who has told us, that " *By Grace* we are *saved* through
" *Faith*; and that not of *ourselves*; it is the
" *Gift* of God: Not of *Works*, lest any Man
" should boast;" I say, the same Holy Spirit immediately assures us, that " We are his
" Workmanship, *created* in *Christ Jesus* un-
" to *good Works*, which God hath before
" *ordained*, that we should *walk in them* (b)."
Therefore, if we *walk not* in *good Works*, do we not contradict the very Reason for which we were *created* anew in *Christ Jesus?* Such a Behaviour is so expressly contrary to our *New Creation* in *Christ*, that nothing can be more manifest or evident. But now, only to mention one Passage more.—We are not only directed to *add to our Faith*—*Virtue*—*Knowledge*—*Temperance*—*Patience*—*Godliness*—*Brotherly-Kindness* and *Charity*; but moreover, these Things are to *be in us and abound:* And it is declared, that *He that lacketh these*
Things

(a) Tit. ii. 11—14. Ch. iii, 8.
(b) Ephes. ii. 8—10.

Things is blind; and *hath forgotten that he was purged from his old Sins* (a).

Would to God, that such as expect to be finally *saved by* an *empty Faith*, would lay these Things seriously to Heart!

E. I take it, that our Church does not give the least Encouragment to such a *dead Faith*.

P. You judge perfectly right: let us only hear in what Manner she describes *true Faith*.

—" This is the *true, lively*, and *unfeigned*
" *Christian Faith*, and is not in the Mouth
" and outward Profession only, but it *liveth*
" and *stirreth* inwardly in the *Heart*. And
" this Faith is not without *Hope* and *Trust* in
" God, nor without the *Love* of *God* and of
" *our Neighbours*, nor without the *Fear of*
" *God*, nor without the *Desire* to hear God's
" Word, and to follow the same, in eschew-
" ing Evil, and doing gladly *all good Works*.
—" [It] is also *moved* through *continual As-*
" *sistance* of the *Spirit of God* to serve and
" and please him, to keep his Favour, to
" fear his Displeasure, to continue his obedi-
" ent Children, shewing Thankfulness again
" by observing or keeping his Command-
" ments, and that freely, for *true Love*
" chiefly, and not for dread of Punishment,
" or love of temporal Reward; considering
" how clearly, without Deservings, we *have*
" received his Mercy and Pardon freely (b)."

—Thus

(a) 2 St Peter i. 5, 9.
(b) Hom. of Faith, Part I. p. 19, 20.

—— Thus does our Church express herself. And thus easily may you know the Difference betwixt a *living* and a *dead* Faith. None can be deceived, but *Hypocrites*, or Men notoriously *careless* and *negligent*. And it is no wonder, if either they, who value *not* their Salvation, should miss of it: Or if such as love to *deceive*, should themselves be fatally *deceived*.

E. I see nothing is wanting to discern the Difference, but an honest and attentive Mind. —— But now, since a thorough Conversion seems, at least in habitual Sinners, to be generally a long and laborious Work; what can we think of those numbers of remarkable *Convictions*, and those many sudden *Conversions*, which of late Years we have heard of, not only in *England* and *Scotland*, but in the remotest Parts of his Majesty's Dominions in *America* (a)? They seem to me too strange and surprizing to be true.

P. Though, my dear Friend, it would be the very Height of Madness and Presumption for Sinners to continue in Sin, in Expectation of so miraculous a Change; yet as we should be exceedingly cautious how we presume to limit the Almighty, since *His Judgments are unsearchable, and his Ways past finding out* (b); so when we have such abundant Evidence of the Facts themselves, it would

---

(a) See the Reverend Mr *Wesley*'s and Mr *Whitefield*'s Accounts; and those from *Scotland* and *America*, in the *New England Christian History*.

(b) Rom. xi. 33.

would argue a furprizing Difpofition towards *doubting*, to refufe giving credit to fuch a number of concurrent Teftimonies. But then, befides, when we meet with feveral Inftances of a like Nature in the *Holy Scripture* (*a*), this demonftrates that the Thing is not entirely new; but only a Revival of what was at the Beginning. And indeed, it is not unreafonable to fuppofe that God would before the End of Time, revive his firft Work, and give new Life to *expiring Chriftianity*, in a way *uncommon, miraculous,* and *aftonifhing*. If it fhould be objected, that thofe ancient Inftances were only of *Jews* and *Gentiles* converted to the Faith of *Chrift*; whereas thefe modern ones are of *Chriftians* fuppofed to be converted from a *dead* Faith, and *dead* Works;—I fay, if any fhould object this Difference; I would defire them to confider, whether all *fuch Chriftians* do not equally want to have their *Eyes opened*; to be *turned from Darknefs to Light*; and *from the Power of Satan unto God?* Whether they do not equally ftand in need of *Repentance*; and a living *Faith* in the Blood of *Jefus?* and whether, without thefe, either of them can receive *Forgivenefs of Sins*; or *Inheritance amongft them which are fanctified by Faith which is in him* (*b*)?

And

(*a*) Acts ii. 37—41, 47. Ch. iv. 4. Ch. v. 14. Ch. ix. 1—20. Ch. xi. 20, 21. Ch. xiii. 12, 48. Ch. xiv. 1. Ch. xvi. 5, 14, 15, 29—34. Ch. xvii. 34. Ch. xviii. 8. Ch. xix. 17—20.

(*b*) Acts xxvi. 18—20. Ch. xx. 21. Ch. viii. 22, 23. Rom. iii. 24, 25. Ch. v. 1. Heb. ix. 14.

And when we further reflect, that God has given our holy Lord *the Heathen for his Inheritance, and the uttermost Part of the Earth for his Possession* (a); that the whole *Jewish* Nation shall be *converted* (b), and the whole World bow down before the Scepter of *Christ*; and when we consider the present melancholy degenerate State of *Christianity*;—I say, when we lay these Things together, can it seem strange, if, whilst God *restores* his divine Gospel where it is just *departing*, and prepares to bring about those other amazing Events, he should *clothe himself* with a more *visible Majesty* than ordinary, and once more *shew Wonders in the Heavens, and in the Earth* (c)?

To these glorious Times the Evangelical Prophet most evidently alludes, where he foretels, that *the Earth shall be full of the Knowledge of the Lord, as the Waters cover the Sea* (d). That famous Prophecy, in all its Parts and whole Extent, has been hitherto but very imperfectly fulfilled (e); and therefore still remains to be entirely accomplished. But before this *Kingdom of Righteousness* can be set up, how many stubborn Enemies of *Christ* must be *broken to Pieces* (f)? To so very awful a Season, we may well apply the Words of the same Prophet, — *Enter into*

(a) Psalm. ii. 8.   Rom. xi. 11, 12, 15, 23—32.
(b) Rev. ii. 15.   (c) Joel ii. 30.
(d) Isaiah xi. 9.   (e) Ver. 6—9.
(f) Psalm ii. 9—12. Psalm cx. 1 Cor. xv. 24, 25.
Ephes. i. 22. Rev. ii. 26, 27. Ch. vi. 2. Ch. xix. 15.

into the Rock, and hide thee in the Dust, for fear of the Lord, and for the Glory of his Majesty. The lofty looks of Man shall be humbled, and the Haughtiness of Men shall be bowed down, and the Lord alone shall be exalted in that Day (a).

So that whether we consider *Christ* as *conquering* (b) his Friends, or his Enemies; whether as subduing the Hearts of the former by his divine Grace, and *plucking them as a Brand out of the Fire* (c); or whether as trampling under Foot those who *will not have him to reign over them* (d); in either of these Views, whenever that solemn time is come for the full Accomplishment of these Things, we may reasonably suppose, that such a Display of the Sovereign Power of *Christ* will be quite out of the ordinary Course of Things. Nor will I take upon me to say, that our holy Lord had no View to this State of the World, when he thus addresses himself to *Nathanael*;--*Hereafter you shall see Heaven open, and the Angels of God ascending and descending upon the Son of Man* (e).

So that you find, my dear *Eugenius*, I should not be surprized, if we should live to see much *stranger* Things than we have hitherto seen.

However, as to the amazing manner of *Conviction*, and the Suddenness or Slowness of *Conversion*;

(*a*) Isaiah ii. 10, 11. (*b*) Rev. vi. 2.
(*c*) Zechar. iii. 2. (*d*) St Luke xix. 27.
(*e*) St John i. 51.

Converſion; this ſpiritual Work of God, upon the Soul, muſt be left to God only. — *I will work*, ſays the Amighty, *and who ſhall let it* (a)?

And again, by the ſame Prophet, — *It ſhall come to paſs, that before they call, I will anſwer; and whilſt they are yet ſpeaking, I will hear* (b).

However, let none harden themſelves in Sin: For though the Spirit of God *will reprove*, or *convince the World of Sin* (c), whether they will or not; yet a thorough and laſting Converſion requires their own Concurrence (d). The Holy Spirit expreſsly commands Men to *give Diligence to make their Calling and Election ſure:* And to *work out their own Salvation with Fear and Trembling* (e).

E. But may not an Objection lie againſt the Nature of the Work itſelf? May it not be ſaid, that ſuch Perſons are *deluded*, if not *poſſeſſed?*

P. It may undoubtedly be ſo ſaid: For what is it, my good Friend, that ſome Men *cannot* ſay? But then, if any one ſhould viſibly ſee the *Fruits of the Spirit of God*, where before he ſaw little except the *Works of the Devil*;

(a) Iſaiah xliii. 13.   (b) Iſaiah lxv. 24.
(c) St John xvi. 8.
(d) St Matth. xxvi. 41.   St Mark xiii. 37.   St Luke xxi. 34, 36. Ch. xxii. 46. St John xv. 1—10. 1 Cor. ix. 27. Ch. x. 12. 2 Cor. xi. 3. Epheſ. vi. 11—18. 1 Theſſ. iii. 5. Heb xii. 15. 1 St Pet. v 8, 9. 2 St Pet. i. 4—9. Rev. iii. 11, 12. Ch. xxii. 11—19.
(e) 2 St Pet. i. 10, 11. Philip. ii. 12, 13.

Devil; would you not think that Person under a strange *Delusion*, who could not plainly discern the *Finger of God?*

E. I really think, I should.

P. Or if a Person of unquestionable Reputation should declare this, upon his own certain Knowledge, might not such an Account, at least, seem to merit a very favourable Attention?

E. I must own, it would. But now, leaving this Digression, which was owing to my Curiosity, I beg to know what a Penitent Sinner must do, who cannot yet find *that Faith* wrought in him, which speaks Peace and Comfort to the Soul?

P. He must pray for it, with great Constancy, Humility, and Patience; and persevere in *bringing forth Fruits meet for Repentance*, to the best of his Abilities (*a*). And it may be great Encouragement for such to consider, that when the *Prodigal was yet a great way off, his Father saw him, and had Compassion, and ran, and fell on his Neck and kissed him* (*b*).

But then, let it be well attended to, that the *Son* was *returning* and *going on, till* his *Father met him* (*c*). For had he, after his Resolution to *arise and go to his Father*, either *changed* his Mind, or *stopped short* in his Journey

———

(*a*) St Matth. ii. 8. St Luke viii. 15. Ch. xviii. 1. Ch. xxi. 19. 2 Thess. iii. 5. Heb. x. 36, 37. St James i. 3, 4. Ch. iv. 6—10. St Mark xiii. 13.

(*b*) St Luke xv. 20.   (*c*) Ver. 18—20.

ney home, or returned to his *Swine* again, he and his *Father* had not then met. And therefore let the Penitent go on forwards, till he *meets* with his *Heavenly Father*; who, at the properest Time and Season, will certainly *fall on his Neck and kiss him.* But, in the mean while, he may be satisfied, he is in the sure Way *to obtain Salvation by our Lord* Jesus Christ (*a*). He may be assured, that God will *look to him, who is poor and of a contrite Heart; and who trembles at his Word* (*b*). God will not despise *the Day of small Things,* nor *the Works of his own Hands* (*c*). But *He, which hath begun a good Work in us, will perform it unto the Day of* Jesus Christ (*d*).

Him that cometh to me, says the holy *Jesus, I will in no wise cast out* (*e*).

He was *sent to bind up the broken-hearted, ——and to comfort all that mourn* (*f*). That God, *whose Name is holy,——dwells with him that is of a contrite and humble Spirit, to revive the Spirit of the Humble, and to revive the Heart of the contrite ones——I create the Fruit of the Lips; Peace, Peace, to him that is far off, and to him that is near, saith the Lord, and I will heal him* (*g*).

Thus will *the God of Hope,* at the best and wisest Season, *fill* every true Penitent, *with all Joy and Peace in believing, that they may abound*

(*a*) 1 Thess. v. 9.   (*b*) Isaiah lxvi. 2.
(*c*) Zechariah iv. 10.   Psalm cxxxviii. 8.
(*d*) Philip. i. 6.   (*e*) St John vi. 37.
(*f*) Isaiah lxi. 1, 2.   (*g*) Ch. lvii. 15—19.

abound in Hope, through the Power of the Holy Ghost (*a*).

He will, when his own adorable Wisdom judges it best, thus discover himself to the Soul of every sincerely returning Sinner: For he is the same *God of Hope and Peace* through *Christ*, that he ever was (*b*). And therefore as he has already done to others; so will he vouchsafe to every proper Object *the Spirit of Adoption, whereby they cry, Abba, Father*: And, at the properest time, *his Spirit will bear witness with their Spirit, that they are the Children of God* (*c*).

But let them *continue instant in Prayer: Praying always with all Prayer and Supplication* (*d*). Let them not be *wearied or faint in their Minds: For yet a little while, and he that shall come, will come, and will not tarry* (*e*).

These ought surely to be powerful Motives, to encourage us to persevere in *the patient waiting for Christ* (*f*).

However, it is evident, that the *Business of Salvation* is *no slight* Affair. And the Reason may be plainly perceived, why the Holy Spirit commands us to *work out our Salvation with Fear and Trembling* (*g*), and to *give Diligence to make our Calling and Election sure* (*h*). You find it is a *great Work*, and that

---

(*a*) Rom. xv. 13.　　(*b*) Heb. xiii. 20, 21.
(*c*) Rom. viii. 15, 16.
(*d*) Rom. xii. 12. Ephes. vi. 18.
(*e*) Heb. xii. 3. Ch. x. 37.　　(*f*) 2 Thess. iii. 5.
(*g*) Phil. ii. 12.　　(*h*) 2 St Pet. i. 10.

that *great Diligence* is therefore indispensably necessary: And that a *holy Fear and Concern*, lest we offend God, or *grieve his holy Spirit* (a), will be present to the Mind of every true *Christian*.

But from hence we may stand amazed at those unhappy Persons, who seem to imagine, that *sitting still*, and *doing* of *nothing*, is the best way to *work out their Salvation!* the best way to *give Diligence to make their Calling and Election sure!*

They, who can reconcile these Things,— *Idleness* with *Diligence*; and *doing nothing* with *working*, need not despair of reconciling any Contradiction whatever.

E. *Salvation*, I am sensible, is a *great Work*: And as we must *work it out*; so is it well worth the while, to *give all Diligence to make it sure* to us. I beg now to be instructed how I am to understand that Expression of the Apostle, that *Christ is of God made unto us Sanctification* (b). For I think some have understood it, as if the *Holiness* of *Christ* was so imputed to us, that we needed *none* in our own *Hearts:* But that we were to look only to the *Holiness* which is *in Christ*; without labouring for any *in ourselves*.

P. If you meet, *Eugenius*, with any who talk in this manner, you have great Reason to pity, and to pray for them: And withal, endeavour,

(*a*) Ephes. iv. 30.   (*b*) 1 Cor. i. 30.

endeavour, in the *Spirit* of *Meekness*, to reclaim them from their Error (*a*).

Christ is made *Sanctification to us*, as he is made to us *Wisdom* and *Redemption*. Not by *imputing* his *Wisdom* and *Redemption* to us; but by making us *wise unto Salvation* (*b*); and redeeming us from the *Dominion*, the *Guilt*, and *Punishment* of *Sin* (*c*); and from the *Power* of the *Grave* (*d*), and of *Satan*, as we have before observed.

And thus is he *made Sanctification unto us:* by procuring for us that *Holy Spirit*, who is to work *that Sanctification* in the Heart, without which we are not qualified for Heaven. For *without Holiness*, [inward real Holiness] *no Man shall see the Lord* (*e*). Having therefore,

---

(*a*) It may not be amiss, for the sake of some Readers, just to observe, that this does not seem to be the Doctrine of *Calvin:* For he says, that God *sanctifies* us, by reforming our *vicious Nature*, by his *Spirit*.—*Justificat nos Deus à Reatu liberando; Sanctificat vitiosam Naturam Spiritu suo reformando.* In 1 Cor. vi. 11.—*Beza*, in his Explanation of *Titus* iii. 7. mentions the *Efficacy of the Spirit in sanctifying of us.*—*Complectitur hic locus, sicut & Rom.* viii 30. *quicquid à Christo consequimur, tum per imputationem, tum per Spiritûs in nobis sanctificandis efficaciam.* And the learned Antagonist of *Arminius* speaks to the same Purpose. — *Christus, qui nos ungit & merito Obedientiæ suæ, & Efficaciâ Spiritûs sui nosmet sanctificantis.*—*Gomarus* in 1 St John ii. 20.

(*b*) Ephes. iii. 17—19. Colos. i. 9. Chap. ii. 2, 3. 2 Tim. iii. 15.

(*c*) Rom. vi. 6, 14, 22. Ch. viii. 2. 2 Cor. v. 18, 19. Ephes. i. 7.

(*d*) Rom. viii. 11, 23. 1 Cor. xv. 54—57. Philip. iii. 21. 1 Thess. iv. 13—16.

(*e*) St Matth. v. 8. Heb. xii. 14.

fore, says the same Apostle, *these Promises, let us cleanse ourselves from all Filthiness of the Flesh and Spirit, perfecting Holiness in the Fear of God* (*a*). Nothing can be more manifest than that St *Paul* speaks here to his Converts of an *universal Sanctification* of *Heart* and *Actions*. He speaks of it, indeed, as of what might be effected by themselves. The Reason is, because they were to labour and pray earnestly for it; and strive to put all Impediments out of the way. But no Words can more fully demonstrate, that *this Holiness* was to be *in* themselves; *in* their *very Souls*, as well as their *outward Practice*.

As he, who hath called you, is Holy,—says the same divine Spirit; *so be ye holy in all manner of Conversation. Because it is written, Be ye holy; for I am holy* (*b*).

Could now the Spirit of God more expresly enjoin *real* Holiness, than when he directs it to be *in all manner of Conversation*; and enforces it from hence; — *because God himself is holy*?

Again, when the same Persons are told, that they *had purified their Souls in obeying the Truth, through the Spirit* (*c*) : and St *Peter* declares that *God had purified the Hearts of the* Gentiles *by Faith* (*d*); what can be meant, but an *actual Purification* of the Heart and Affections?

Moreover,

(*a*) 2 Cor. vii. 1.   (*b*) 1 St Pet. i. 15, 16.
(*c*) Ver. 22.   (*d*) Acts xv. 9.

Moreover, when St *Paul* tells the *Thessalonians*, that *God had from the beginning chosen them to Salvation, through Sanctification of the Spirit, and Belief of the Truth* (a); — What Sanctification can the Apostle mean, but a *real inward Holiness* wrought in their Souls by the Holy Spirit?

And further, when he desires, that *the Lord would stablish their Hearts unblameable in Holiness before God:* And that *the very God of Peace would sanctify them wholly:* And that *their whole Spirit, and Soul and Body, might be preserved blameless unto the coming of our Lord* Jesus Christ (b); I say, when the Apostle thus expresses himself, is it possible to understand him, as if he really did not desire, that they should have any *inward Holiness of Soul* or *Spirit*; but only that they should lay Claim to the *Holiness of Christ*; whilst they themselves were destitute of *all real Holiness within* their own Hearts?

If this be to *stablish* the Heart *in* Holiness; I should be glad to know, what it is to have the Heart *without* Holiness?

I pray God open the Eyes of such Interpreters of the sacred Writings! Be assured, my good Friend, that the great Work of *Sanctification* is of a different Nature. It is an *actual purifying* of the *whole Heart* and
Affections,

(a) 2 Thess. ii. 13.
(b) 1 Thess. iii. 13. 'Ch. v. 23.

Affections, by the Spirit of *Christ*; it is the restoring of the lost Image of God in our Souls; and thus qualifying of us for that State of Blessedness, which none but *holy* Souls are capable of enjoying: And without which, *Christ* is neither our *Wisdom*, nor *Righteousness*, nor *Sanctification*, nor *Redemption*.—Pray hear once more the Words of the Spirit of Truth,——*Every Man that hath this Hope in him* [the Hope of seeing God] *purifieth himself even as he is pure. They that are* Christ's *have crucified the Flesh, with the Affections and Lusts* (a).

E. It seems then, as if a State of *thorough Sanctification* was attainable in this Life. I should be glad to know the Opinion of our Church, with respect to such a State.

P. It is evident, from what has just been mentioned, not only that such a State is *attainable*; but that wretched must be the Fate of that Person who *attains* it *not*. For since he must arrive at it before he can *see God*; where is it, that he must arrive at it, if not in *this World?* The *Romish Church* indeed, as you well know, have found out another Place to attain it in; as the ancient Heathens had done long before:— But I would advise all, who value their Souls, not to trust to the *Purification* of that Place. And therefore

---

(a) 1 St John iii. 2, 3.   Gal. v. 24.   See also 1 St John ii. 6.   2 St Peter iii. 11, 14.

fore since it *must* be *attained* in *this* Life; and and the Holy Spirit is as powerful at one Season as at another; surely the sooner we labour after it, by all the Means of Grace, the sooner we are like to attain it.

It is true, he will not *sanctify* any *unqualified* or *unsuitable* Object; but then if our Want of due Qualifications be owing to ourselves; to our wilful Negligence or Carelessness; we have none to blame but ourselves only Perhaps we are too *fond* of this World; and if not of its *grosser* Vices, yet of its *Follies* and *Vanities*; its *Riches*, *Honours*, or *Pleasures*: Or possibly we have some other *Right-hand*, or *Right-eye*; some darling favourite Sin of the Soul, which we have not the Courage to part with; such as *Pride*, *Wrath*, *Luxury*, *Covetousness*, or the *Praise* of *Men*. Therefore we do not desire, at this Time, to have so *holy* and *heavenly* a Frame of Mind; so *meek* and *lowly* a Heart; so *pious* and *patient* a Soul; so *mortified* and *self-denying* a Spirit (*a*). And consequently we neither labour nor pray for these Things. We may possibly, for Form's sake, put up a Petition, now and then, for all these divine Graces; but as such Prayers proceed not from the Heart (where we have set up some *Idol* or other) is it to be wondered at, that

---

(*a*) St Matth. xi. 29. St Luke ix. 23. 1 Cor. ix. 24—27. Gal. v. 22—26.

that we are anfwered only *according to our Folly?* We are not fit for fuch divine Favours; and therefore they are kept from us. Thus verifying the Words of the Holy Spirit,—*Ye have not, becaufe ye afk not. Ye afk, and receive not; becaufe ye afk amifs* (a).

And now, if this *thorough Sanctification* is what we are to underftand by *finlefs* or *Chriftian Perfection,* it may juftly feem furprizing, that it fhould have been treated as downright *Enthufiafm* or *Madnefs.* The Doctrine itfelf, we have feen, is the Doctrine of the Spirit of God: And it will be eafy to find, that our own Church teaches the fame. For what elfe does fhe mean by the following Petitions? —That " *God would fanctify both our Hearts* " *and Bodies.* (b); That *we may be cleanfed* " *from all our Sins* (c); That *this Day we* " *fall into no Sin* (d); That God would *keep* " *us this Day without Sin.* (e); That *we may* " *be delivered from all the Deceits of the* " *World, the Flefh, and the Devil* (f); That " *we may forfake all worldly and carnal Af-* " *fections* (g); That we may always *ferve* " [God] *in Purenefs of Living and Truth* (b); " That

(a) St James iv. 2, 3. 1 St John v. 21.
(b) Collect 2d following the Bleffing after the Communion. (c) Collect 21ft after Trinity.
(d) Third Collect for Grace. (e) *Te Deum.*
(f) Litany. (g) Collect for St James.
(h) Collect firft Sunday after Eafter. See alfo the Collect for Innocents Day. Exhortation before the Communion, with the Confeffion and Abfolution: And the firft proper Preface.

"That *we may in Heart and Mind* ascend
"[into the Heavens] *and with* [Christ] *con-*
"*tinually dwell* (a); That God would *grant*
"*us the Spirit to think and do always such*
"*Things as be rightful* (b); And *that we*
"*may perfectly love* [God] (c); And *walk*
"*before him in Holiness and Righteousness all*
"*our Days* (d)."

Surely this *perfect Love of God*; this continual *walking in Holiness and Righteousness*; this *Heavenly Frame* of Heart and Mind; this continual *thinking* and *doing* what is *right*; this *constant serving* of God in *Pureness of living*; this forsaking *all worldly and carnal Affections*; the being *Day by Day* preserved *from Sin*; the being *cleansed* from *all* of them; and the being *sanctified* both in *Heart* and *Body*; I say, surely these Things are *attainable*, in the Opinion of our Church, or she would never have thus petitioned for them. But what do all these Things amount to, if not to a State of *thorough Sanctification* of the Flesh and Spirit?

If all would heartily set themselves to arrive at this blessed State, as it is the plain Duty and Interest of all to do; it is of little Importance, whether they call it *Holiness*, or *Perfection*, or by any other Name.

(a) Collect for Ascension Day.
(b) Collect for the Ninth Sunday after Trinity.
(c) Collect following the Lord's Prayer in the Communion-Service. (d) General Thanksgiving.

E. I see plainly the indispensable Necessity of *universal Holiness* in this Life; which makes me even tremble to think, how far removed I am from it.—But since it has been objected, that the *Doctrine* of *Perfection* is attended with *some dangerous Consequences*, I should be glad to be satisfied with respect to these Objections.

The first is, that *it encourages Pride*.

Secondly, that *it cuts off all Dependence on* Christ, *the Fountain of all Grace*.

Thirdly, that *it totally sets aside the Way of Access to God; which is by* Jesus Christ.

And, fourthly, that *it sets aside Prayer, especially those two great Parts of it, Confession and Petition* (a).

P. These are great Objections indeed! But if it should appear, that they are very ill-founded, they must of course come to nothing. But, first, since the *holy Angels* themselves appear to have fallen by *Pride* (b); it can be no Wonder, if a very *holy* Man should, for want of due Care and Watchfulness, fall into the same *spiritual Snare:* But then it should be remembered, that *this Pride* is *no Part* of his *Holiness*; nor any Reason, why he should not labour for a State of *universal Holiness*. For since *without Holiness no Man shall see the Lord* (c);—*Holiness* we must have,

(a) The *Perfectionists Examined*, p. 7, 8, &c. by *William Fleetwood*, Gent.
(b) 2 St Pet. ii. 4. St Jude 6. 1 Tim. iii. 6.
(c) Heb. xii. 14.

have, let Men raife never fuch *powerful* Objections againſt it.

Can any *Chriſtian* in his Senſes think it a ſufficient Reaſon, why he ſhould *wallow in Sin*, becauſe then he cannot *pride* himſelf in his *Holineſs* or *Perfection?* Surely to be *pure in Heart* and *poor in Spirit*, are very confiſtent States.

But, ſecondly, as to *its cutting off all Dependence on* Chriſt, *the Fountain of all Grace*; I affirm, on the contrary, that a *truly ſanctified* Soul will ſee its Want of *Chriſt* every Day more evidently.——The more *holy* are our Hearts, the more *humble* are they like to be, and the more *earneſt* our Deſires after greater Supplies of Grace. And ſuch Deſires will of courſe ſend us to *him*, through whom alone they can be ſupplied.

As to the third Objection, that *it totally ſets aſide the Way of Acceſs to God, which is through* Chriſt. — Surely, if this was a *neceſſary* Conſequence of a *thorough Sanctification*, St *Paul* had never directed the *Corinthians* to *perfect Holineſs in the Fear of God* (*a*). Nor prayed, that *God would ſanctify* the *Theſſalonians wholly* : Nor that their *whole Spirit, and Soul, and Body might be preſerved blameleſs* (*b*). Nor had St *Peter* exhorted thoſe *Chriſtians* to be *holy in all manner of Converſation* ; nor to be *diligent*, that they might be *found of God without*

(*a*) 2 Cor. vii. 1.   (*b*) 1 Theſs. v. 23.

without Spot and blameless (*a*).— I say, if a thorough *Sanctification totally set aside the going to God through* Christ, these inspired Apostles had never thus laboured to bring *Christians* to such a State. Because the thus approaching God is as much the indispensable Duty of the greatest *Saint* upon Earth, as of the greatest *Sinner*. This is what I shall endeavour to establish very evidently (*b*); but first proceed to consider the remaining Objection; *viz.* That *this State sets aside Prayer*; *especially these two great Parts of it, Confession and Petition.*— In Opposition to which, I must beg leave to assert, that there is none so *holy*; none so *perfect*; but he must both be *established in the Faith*; and *abound therein with Thanksgiving* (*c*). He must still *grow in Grace*; and *in the Knowledge of our Lord and Saviour* Jesus Christ (*d*). He must be still *adding to his Faith, Virtue*; *to Virtue, Knowledge*; *to Knowledge, Temperance*; *to Temperance, Patience*; *to Patience, Godliness*; *to Godliness, Brotherly Kindness*; *and to Brotherly Kindness, Charity*: And *these Things must be in him, and abound* (*e*). He must sincerely strive to *love the Lord his God, with all his Heart, and with all his Soul, and with all his Mind, and with all his Strength*; and even his worst Enemies, as *Christ* loved him (*f*).

Here

(*a*) 1 St Peter i. 15. 2 Epistle iii. 14.
(*b*) See Page 70. (*c*) Colos. ii. 7. Rom. i. 17.
(*d*) 2 St Pet. iii. 18. (*e*) 2 St Peter i. 5—8.
(*f*) St Mark xii. 30, 31. St Matth. v. 44. St John xiii. 34. Rom. v. 6, 8, 10. 1 St John iv. 11, 12.

Here is then abundant Matter for every Day's *Confeſſion* and *Petition*; and for every Hour's too.—Where is that *Saint* upon Earth, who can ſay, he has ſpent the preceding Day, or even Hour, with *all* that *Care*, and *Watchfulneſs*, and *Diligence*; and with all that *Patience*, and *Self-denial*, and *Chriſtian Love*, and *univerſal Charity*; and that he has improved himſelf as much in *Faith*, and *Grace*, and the *Knowledge of Chriſt*; and in the *Fear*, and *Knowledge*, and *Love* of God, as it was *poſſible* for him to do? So that here is ſufficient Matter to *confeſs*; and ſufficient to *aſk Pardon* for. Here is ſufficient Cauſe to *petition* for further Supplies of divine Aid; in order to make further Advances in the *divine Life*: And here is abundant Reaſon for perpetual *Humiliation*. Or ſhall we ſay, *Eugenius*, it is better for Men to *continue in Sin, that Grace may abound* (a); that ſo they may have *more* to *confeſs*; and *more* to *petition* for?

E. If we are *only unprofitable Servants*, even *after we have done all*; ſurely here alone is enough to *humble* us. And therefore I pray God make me always *holy* and *humble*, *watchful* and *diligent*.

P. Go on, my Friend, as I truſt you have begun; and the Holy Spirit will not be wanting to aſſiſt you. It is worthy of Obſervation, that holy *Job* was never ſo *humble*,
as

(a) Rom. vi. 1.

as when he had the clearest Discoveries of a *Holy God.*—He then *abhorred himself, and repented in Dust and Ashes* (*a*). But I shall now further add a Caution or two, which may still excite even the most *perfect Christian* to perpetual Care, and Vigilance, and Humility.

And, first, it must always be remembered, that notwithstanding *Holiness* be indispensably necessary to the Enjoyment of Heaven; yet we are not to look upon the most *holy* or *heavenly Frame* of Spirit; or, in short, upon the most *righteous, pious,* or *charitable* Actions of our whole Lives, as the Cause or Foundation of our Acceptance with God (*b*). We must altogether renounce the *Merit* of these, and only take Shelter in the *Merits* of *Christ*. For though we must diligently strive after such a Frame of Spirit; and, to our Power, live in the Exercise of such Actions: And though they are entitled to a great and bountiful Reward (*c*), through the Free Grace of God in *Christ*; yet *when we have done all,* (as you have just observed) *we are but unprofitable Servants* (*d*); we have *nothing*, but what we have *received*; 1 Cor. iv. 7. therefore neither *we* nor our *Service* can *merit* any thing. All our *spiritual Sacrifices* are only acceptable

---

(*a*) Job xlii. 5, 6.   (*b*) 2 Tim. i. 9.   Tit. iii. 5.
(*c*) St Matth. v. 8.   2 St Peter i. 4.   St Matth. xxv. 34—46. Phil. iv. 18.   Heb. vi. 10.   Chap. xiii. 16. Rev. xiv. 13.   (*d*) St Luke xvii. 10.

acceptable to God, by Jesus Christ (*a*). If the *Prayers of the greatest Saint* be not *offered with Incense by* Christ *himself*, they will no more *ascend up before God* (*b*), than the Prayers of the greatest *Sinner*. *Aaron* was, in this Particular, a remarkable Type of our great *High Priest*; in that he was to *bear* [or take away] *the Iniquity of the holy Things* (*c*). And if the *Iniquity of our holy Things* be not cleansed by the *Blood of sprinkling* (*d*), [let the most sanctified Person think on this] they will not prove *an Odour of a sweet Smell, a Sacrifice acceptable, well-pleasing to God* (*e*). So that it will always become us, when we look upon our own *righteous* Actions, as considered in themselves, to say in the Language of the *Prophet,—All our Righteousnesses are as filthy Rags* (*f*).

Let us remember, that *Christ*, and he alone, is the *Author, meritorious Cause*, and *Foundation* of our *Acceptance* and *Reconciliation* with God. And consequently on *him*, and his *Merits*, and the *Free Grace* of God *in him*, we must altogether rely and depend (*g*). Otherwise we act directly contrary to the great

(*a*) 1 Peter ii. 5.   (*b*) Rev. viii. 3, 4.
(*c*) Exod. xxviii. 38.
(*d*) Heb. xii. 24.   1 Peter ii. 5.   Rev. vii. 13, 14.
(*e*) Phil. iv. 18.   Rom. xv. 16.   (*f*) Isai. lxiv. 6.
(*g*) 2 Cor. v. 18, 19.   Ephes. ii. 13—18.   Col. iii. 11.   Heb. v. 9.   Ch. xii. 2.   Rom. iii. 24.   Ch. v. 8. 1 St John iv. 9, 10.

great inspired Apostle, who desired only to *be found in Christ*; *not having*, says he, *mine own Righteousness, which is of the Law; but that which is through the Faith of* Jesus Christ; *the Righteousness which is of God by Faith* (*a*). He disclaimed all Merit in his own Performances, and rested solely in the Merits of *Christ*. He desired altogether to rely on the *Righteousness of* Christ, justified *through Faith in him*; and possessed of all the other blessed Fruits and Consequences of what *Christ* had done and suffered; that so *Christ* might be to him *Wisdom*, and *Righteousness*, and *Sanctification*, and *Redemption* (*b*). This was the Foundation he built upon; and if we build upon any other, it will certainly fail us. *For other Foundation can no Man lay, than that is laid; which is* Jesus Christ (*c*).

However, Secondly, Men are not to imagine, that they are hereby excused from the Performance of any good Work in their Power. In particular, they are not excused from that Part of *pure and undefiled Religion*, which consists in *visiting the Fatherless and Widows in their Affliction, and keeping themselves unspotted from the World* (*d*).

Let the *Rich* ever bear in Mind the charge given by the Spirit of God, not only——
" That they *do Good*, but that they be *rich*
" in *good Works*, ready to distribute, *willing*
" to

(*a*) Philip. iii. 9.   (*b*) 1 Cor. i. 30.
(*c*) Ch. iii. 11.   (*d*) St James i. 27.

"to communicate (*a*)." So that it is not complying with this divine Command, unless such Persons *willingly*, and *readily*, and *abundantly* communicate out of their large Possessions. How else can they be *rich in* these *good Works?* How else can they *sow bountifully?* or pay a just Regard to that divine Promise, that *he which soweth bountifully, shall reap also bountifully* (*b*)? But after what manner is it, that these divine Precepts are now generally complied with? or how many does this Promise seem now to influence? Are *stately Buildings*, or *costly Furniture*, or *rich Attire*, or *luxurious Tables*, or a *splendid Equipage*, or the *hoarding* up of *Treasure*;— Are these any *Proof*, that Men are governed by the Gospel of *Christ*; or that they are led by his Spirit (*c*)? Is it thus, they *lay up Treasures in Heaven*; *set their Affections on Things above*; or *demonstrate*, that they *are rich towards God?* That they neither *love the World*, nor the *Things of the World*; nor are *conformed to it?* However, though the one may be no *direct* Proof or Demonstration of the other; yet Men seem to have found out so many *ingenious* Solutions of *difficult* Texts of Scripture, and to have such a peculiar Happiness

(*a*) 1 Tim. vi. 17, 18.   (*b*) 2 Cor. ix. 6.
(*c*) I will not venture to say, they are a *direct Proof* of the *contrary*; but, considering the real State of the World, they furnish out but too strong a *Presumption*, that Mens Hearts are not much influenced by the *Spirit of Christ*.

pineſs in *ſoftening* all its *hard Sayings*, that the *narrow Way*, *which leadeth unto Life*, is become ſufficiently *wide* for a *covetous Heart*, a *carnal* Mind, or a *worldly* Spirit.

I do not pretend to refer you to any particular *Commentary*, where ſuch Expoſitions are expreſsly taught or maintained; but I refer you to the Practice and Behaviour of too many Profeſſors of *Chriſtianity*; who could never be ſo thoroughly ſatisfied with themſelves, unleſs they explained away the many *ſevere* Paſſages of the Goſpel of *Chriſt*.

But how different, my good Friend, is the Deſcription, which the great Apoſtle gives of the *Chriſtians* of *Macedonia?* That the *Abundance of their Joy*, and *their deep Poverty, abounded unto the Riches of their Liberality!* And this even *in a great Trial of Affliction* (a)!

Let this, my dear *Eugenius*, be a Leſſon for you: And though your *deep Poverty* cannot, yet let your *affluent Fortune* abundantly diſcover a true *Chriſtian* Spirit, by a *chearful and rich Liberality*, to ſupply the ſpiritual and temporal Wants of Mankind. Be aſſured, my good Friend, that when the *gaudy Scenes* of Life are over, as they are certainly every Day vaniſhing, you will then find, by a joyful Experience, what the Lord *Jeſus* long ſince declared,— that *it is more bleſſed to give than to receive* (b). And you will then plainly diſcern the Folly of thoſe, who, to excuſe their

(a) 2 Cor. viii. 1, 2.   (b) Acts xx. 35.

[63]

their Neglect of being *rich towards God* (*a*), have, under the Notion of *providing for their own*, heaped much Treasure together for aggrandizing their Families. Thus is the Gospel of *Christ* obeyed!

E. But has not the great Apostle declared, that *if any provide not for his own, and especially for those of his own House, he hath denied the Faith, and is worse than an Infidel* (*b*)?

P. He has so. And though nothing seems plainer, than that the Apostle is there speaking of *Childrens requiting their Parents* (*c*), and not suffering of them, or any other poor Relations, to be a Burden to others; yet I know learned Men, according to Custom, are divided in their Sentiments about this very plain Part of Scripture. However, let the Precept *immediately* relate either to Parents or Children (as most certainly it may be extended to both) yet surely there can be no Dispute, what *sort of Provision* is there commanded: Not certainly a Provision of *Grandeur* and *Luxury*; but of *Things needful for their Support* (*d*). However, though nothing can be more plain than this; yet, I doubt

---

(*a*) St Luke xii. 21.   (*b*) 1 Tim. v. 8.
(*c*) Verse 4.
(*d*) *Ut habeant unde vivant.* Grot. *in loc.*—*Parentes, qui jure suo possunt alimenta à liberis repetere, cæteraque ad vitam necessaria* Hammond *apud Le Clerc.*—In his Commentary he has this Note: Προνοεῖν *hic non est sublevare sollicitâ quâdam providentiâ, priusquam necessitas ulla sit; sed præsenti egestati opem ferre.*

doubt not, this very Passage of Scripture is often brought to vindicate a Practice, which it was never designed to give the least Countenance to.

E. But then, does not the same Apostle affirm, that *the Parents are to lay up for the Children* (a)? And I think the original Word is to *lay up Treasure* (b).

P. It is, my dear Friend, the same Word which our blessed Lord uses, where he commands us *not to lay up for ourselves Treasures upon Earth, but to lay up Treasures in Heaven* (c). However, if we allow there is a perfect Consistency in the Precepts of the Holy Spirit, we must grant, that we are *so* to lay up Treasures *for our Children,* that we may at the same time *lay up Treasures for ourselves in Heaven.* Now, which seems the likeliest Way to do this?—Is it by being *rich towards God*; by being *rich in good Works*; by ministring *bountifully* to the spiritual and temporal Necessities of Mankind; though by this means we leave our Families O N L Y the *divine Blessing,* and a *moderate* Competency? or is it by relieving the Miseries of others, with a *scanty* Hand; and laying up *such Treasures* for our Children, as may prove so many *Snares* to their Souls? Such as may prove the Occasion of *Pride* and *Vanity,* of *Luxury* and *Extravagance*? Such as may tempt

(a) 2 Cor. xii. 14. (b) Θησαυρίζειν.
(c) St Matth. vi. 19, 20.

Mind, or a corrupt Heart, to
ay in *Riot* or *Gaming*, what
faved many a Perfon from the
/s?

d the World, my dear *Eugenius*,
to *what Ufes* large Fortunes are
plied. And then reflect, whe-
ents, as *treafure* up *fo much* for
s, and *fo little* for the Suffering
kind, — whether they are *laying
elves Treafures in Heaven?* And
y do not fometimes *lay up* for
n a *Curfe* rather than a *Blefsing?*

the moft bountiful and moft
rfons muft not value themfelves
itable Actions, nor truft to *them*;
only. But now, fince he has
hat *he is the Way, and the Truth,*
and that *no Man cometh unto
t by him:* And affured his Dif-
vhatfoever they fhould afk in his
ould do it (a): — Since we are
by the Holy Spirit, that *what-
in Word or Deed, to do all in the
Lord* Jefus, *giving Thanks to God
r by him* (b): And according to
nd, the Apoftle thus expreffes
nto him be Glory in the Church by
throughout all Ages, World with-
— Again, fince the fame Holy
Spirit

iv. 6, 13, 14. Ch. xvi. 23, 24.
. 17.   (c) Ephes. iii. 21.

Spirit has assured us, that *we are accepted in the Beloved* (*a*); and that *Christ is able to save them to the uttermost that come unto God by him; seeing he ever liveth to make Intercession for them* (*b*). And moreover, that *through him we have an Access by one Spirit unto the Father* (*c*) :—I say, for all these Reasons, it appears to me most abundantly evident, that no Person, none excepted, can have *Access to the Father* but only *by Christ*. I know the Holy Spirit mentions a Time, when *Christ shall have delivered up the Kingdom to God, even the Father*; and when *God shall be all in all* (*d*).

However, *that Time* is not yet come. It is not *here*; but *hereafter*. The utmost we can understand by those Words, is, That when *Christ* has subdued all his Enemies; then his *mediatory Kingdom* will be surrendered into the Hands of God.—*Christ* indeed shall reign as *King* for ever and ever; and all his Saints with him: But he seems not then to reign as *Mediator*, or *Intercessor*; because that great Work will then be fully ended and completed (*e*).

But still, in the present State of Things, *Christ* is our *Priest*, and *Prophet*, and *Mediator*; as well as *King*: *Christ is all, and in all*; and

(*a*) Ephes. i. 6.   (*b*) Heb. vii. 25.
(*c*) Ephes. ii. 18.   (*d*) 1 Cor. xv. 24, 28.
(*e*) See the learned Bishop *Pearson* on the Creed, p. 101, 104, 152, 153, 283. Sixth Edition.

and *filleth all in all* (*a*): And therefore we must not presume to approach the Father, but *through* the Son: Our Prayers and Praises cannot be *acceptable to God*, but *by Jesus Christ* (*b*). *By him therefore*, says the great Apostle, *let us offer the Sacrifice of Praise to God continually* (*c*). And now, as this is the indispensable Duty of every *Christian*, so the Doctrine of *universal Holiness* is far enough from being an Enemy to it.

Thirdly, since a *Christian wrestles not* [only] *against Flesh and Blood*; *but against Principalities, against Powers, against the Rulers of the Darkness of this World, against spiritual Wickedness in high Places*; therefore they have need enough to *put on the whole Armour of God, that they may be able to stand against the Wiles of the Devil* (*d*). He is a very subtle Adversary, and knows our weak Side: And, unless we follow our holy Lord's Directions, he will both assault us, where we lie most exposed; and will certainly defeat us (*e*). And therefore let us be ever upon our Guard; and *watch and pray lest we enter into Temptation* (*f*). Whoever imagines he has made such Ad-

vances

(*a*) Colos. iii. 11.   Ephes. i. 23.
(*b*) 1 St Peter ii. 5.   (*c*) Heb. xiii. 15.
(*d*) Ephes. vi. 11, 12.
(*e*) 2 Cor. ii. 11.   Ch. xi. 3, 14.   1 Thess. iii. 5. 1 St Peter v. 8.   Rev. ii. 24.
(*f*) St Matth. xxvi. 41.   St Mark xiii. 37.   St Luke xxi. 36.

vances in Religion, that such Cautions are unnecessary, is in the utmost Danger of feeling the Effects of his own Rashness, Presumption, and Self-sufficiency.

The greatest Proficient in the School of *Christ* ought frequently to reflect on that solemn Caution, *Thou standest by Faith. Be not high-minded, but fear* (*a*). Nor are those other Directions of the same Apostle less needful for him, *Let him that thinketh he standeth, take heed lest he fall* (*b*). He is but yet in a Probation-State; and therefore must constantly look to himself. The *whole* Life of a *Christian* upon Earth, is but one continued Journey towards *Heaven*; and therefore he must daily *forget those Things which are behind, and reach forth unto those Things which are before; and press toward the Mark for the Prize*

(*a*) Rom. xi. 20.

(*b*) 1 Cor. x. 12. If any one should imagine that these Directions cannot belong to him; because he does not only *think* that he *stands*; but knows for a Certainty that he does so;—such a Person may be pleased to observe, that there is not the least Necessity to suppose the Apostle here applies himself to *vain, conceited* Persons, who only *fancied* they *stood fast*, whilst they were just *falling:* For at Verse 15. he says, he *speaks as to wise Men.* So that he appears plainly to intimate, that *without due Care and Watching, the best might fall.* And moreover, it is to be observed, that the Verb δοκεῖν is often an Expletive. See Mark x. 42. St Luke viii. 18. 1 Cor. vii. 40. Ch. xi. 16. Heb. iv. 1. See also our learned *Gataker* in his *Cinnus*, Ch. i. p. 37—40. And *Hammond* on St Matth. iii. 9.

Prize of the High Calling of God in Christ Jesus (*a*). The most *advanced*, and most *improved Christian*, has still *greater Advances* and *higher Improvements* to make; and these require constant Care, and Prayer, and Watchfulness.

For though every Day *his Salvation is nearer, than when he* first *believed* (*b*); yet he must remember, that *he that shall endure unto the End, the same shall be saved* (*c*). —— So that if he would *receive the Prize*, he must *so run that he may obtain* (*d*). But if he stops short in this *Christian* Race; or fancies it is over, before he has *finished his Course* (*e*); that is, before he has finished his Days in his Lord's Service; and his Lord calls upon him to give an Account of his *Talents* and *Stewardship* (*f*);—I say, if he does this, I fear he does not *so run as to obtain the Prize*.— The holy Apostle, after twenty Years painful *Running, Hunger, Thirst*, and *Nakedness*, and *Sufferings* of *every kind*, yet left not off to *run*, and *fight*, and *mortify*. Let *all Christians* hear his own Words, and learn to imitate.

I therefore so run, says this holy Man, *not as uncertainly: So fight I, not as one that beateth the Air: But I keep under my Body, and bring it into Subjection; lest, that by any Means,*

E *when*

(*a*) Philip. iii. 13, 14.   (*b*) Rom. xiii. 11.
(*c*) St Matth. xxiv. 13.   (*d*) 1 Cor. ix. 24.
(*e*) Acts xx. 24.
(*f*) St Matth. xxv. 13—19. St Luke xii. 35—44.

when I have preached to others, I myself should be a Cast-away (a).———Surely, if this was the Behaviour of one, who had been a faithful, laborious, and persecuted Soldier of *Jesus Christ* for so many Years; and who had *the Power of* Christ *resting upon him* (b); what *Christian* can think, that the same *Care*, and *Vigilance*, and *Self-denial*, are unnecessary for himself?—But further, his Directions to the *Hebrews* are highly deserving of notice. — *Looking diligently lest any Man fall from the Grace of God.* For so the Words are rendered in the Margin; and so they ought to be rendered (c). — Again, after he had told the *Colossians*, that *Christ* had *reconciled them, in the Body of his Flesh through Death, to present them holy, and unblameable, and unreproveable in the Sight* [of God], he then adds these remarkable Words,—*If ye continue in the Faith, grounded and settled, and be not moved away from the Hope of the Gospel* (d).

By the former is evidently imply'd, that without great Care and Circumspection, *Christians* are in certain Danger *of falling from divine Grace.* And by the latter is plainly declared, that the Benefits of Christ's Death would be lost to us, unless we *continued stedfast in the Faith.*

To the same Effect is that solemn Caution of the Son of God to the Church of *Philadelphia,*

(a) 1 Cor. ix. 26, 27.   (b) 2 Cor. xii. 9.
(c) Heb. xii. 15. μή τις ὑστερῶν ἀπὸ τῆς χάριτος τοῦ Θεοῦ.
(d) Coloss. 1. 21—23. See also Heb. iii. 6, 14.

phia,—Hold that fast which thou hast, that no Man take thy Crown (*a*). If that Crown could not be taken, then our Lord uses an Argument to *strike Fear,* where *no Fear* was. But further, he had long before told his Disciples, that *he was the Vine,* and *they the Branches:* But that *every Branch in him, which did not bear Fruit,* his Father would *take away* (*b*). Can any thing now be more manifest, than that a Person, who had been spiritually ingrafted into *Christ,* if he did not bring forth the Fruits of the Gospel, would be cut off as an useless and *withered Branch* (*c*)? I pray God these Reflections may sink deep into the Mind of every Professor of *Christianity*; and cause him to watch diligently his Heart and Actions.

E. May they ever sink deep into mine, in particular.

P. But still I have one Caution more to add; though I trust it will never be necessary as to yourself: And it is, that Men would never fancy themselves *Children of God,* whilst they are plainly indulging themselves in the *Works of the Devil.* The Holy Spirit has abundantly provided against this horrible Delusion; if such unhappy Creatures would not *close their Eyes, lest they should see* (*d*).

Let us attend a Moment to his divine Instructions

(*a*) Rev. iii. 11. See also Ch. xxii. 19.
(*b*) St John xv. 1, 2. (*c*) Verse 4—8. See the Homily of falling from God, Part I. p. 7.
(*d*) St Matth. xiii. 14, 15.

ſtructions.—" *Hereby* we do know that we
" *know him*, if we *keep his Commandments.*
" He that faith, *I know him*, and *keepeth not*
" *his Commandments*, is a *Liar*, and the
" *Truth is not in him.* But whoſo *keepeth*
" *his Word*, in him verily is *the Love of God*
" *perfected*; *hereby* know we that we are *in*
" *him.* He that ſaith, *he abideth in him*,
" *ought himſelf alſo ſo to walk, even as he*
" *walked* (a)."

" Whoſoever abideth in him, *ſinneth not:*
" Whoſoever *ſinneth*, hath not *ſeen him*, nei-
" ther *known him.* Little Children, let no
" Man *deceive* you; he that *doth Righteouſ-*
" *neſs*, is *righteous*, even as He is righteous.
" He that *committeth* Sin, is of the *Devil.*—
" For this Purpoſe the Son of God was ma-
" nifeſted, that he might *deſtroy the Works*
" *of the Devil.*

" Whoſoever is born of God, doth not
" commit Sin; for his Seed remaineth in
" him: And he cannot ſin, becauſe he is
" born of God. In this the *Children of God*
" are manifeſt, and the *Children of the De-*
" *vil:* Whoſoever doth *not Righteouſneſs*, is
" *not of God* (b)."

How plain and expreſs are the Marks here
laid down by the Holy Spirit; by which
Men may judge, whether they belong to God
or not?—He that *belongs to God*, muſt *walk,
even as* Chriſt *himſelf walked.* If we would
know that we are *in him*, we muſt *keep* his
.Com-

(a) 1 St John ii. 6—10.   (b, St John iii. 6—10.

Commandments. He that keeps *not* the *divine Commands, knows not God, as he ought to know. He hath not seen him, neither known him.*

Secondly, he that imagines himself to be *righteous,* without leading a *righteous Life,* is entirely *deceived.*

Thirdly, he that indulges himself in any Sin, is doing the *Work of the Devil,* and so far runs counter to the very Reason, why *Christ was manifested in the Flesh.*

And fourthly, as he that *doth not Righteousness,* is *not of God;* and as *he that committeth Sin, is of the Devil:* Therefore such Men cannot be the *Children of God.* They are not those *living Branches,* which are *ingrafted into Christ;* for these *bring forth much Fruit with Patience and Perseverance;* and labour even to be *filled with the Fruits of Righteousness* (*a*). Thus they give Proof, that *Christ is formed in them;* that *he dwells in their Hearts by Faith;* and that they are *led by his Spirit* (*b*).

Whereas the others are those *fruitless* and *withered Branches,* which, our blessed Lord assures us, are *gathered, and cast into the Fire, and burned. Every Tree,* says the Son of God, *that bringeth not forth good Fruit, is hewn down and cast into the Fire* (*c*). Even those

E 3   that

(*a*) St John xv. 4, 5.   St Luke viii. 15.   Rom. ii. 6, 7.   Phil. i. 11.

(*b*) Gal. ii. 20.   Ch. iv. 10.   Ephes. iii. 17.   Rom. viii. 9, 14.

(*c*) St John xv. 2, 6.   St Matth. vii. 19—21.

that have *prophesied in the Name of* Christ, *worked Miracles,* and *cast out Devils,* will be commanded to *depart from Christ,* if they have been *Workers of Iniquity* (*a*).

How fatally then must those be deluded, who fancy they may safely indulge in the *Works of the Devil*; because, as they imagine, *Sins are not imputed to the Children* of *God* (*b*). I pray God preserve every one from such dreadful *Delusions!* For if a vicious Person or Hypocrite should persuade himself that he was a *Child of God*, and that therefore *his Sins would not be imputed to him*; so unhappy a Creature is in a fair Way to sin on, till his Eyes open *in the Place of Torments.*—*If the Light that is in thee be Darkness, how great is that Darkness* (*c*)!

E. I know there is a famous Text, which is often appealed to upon such Occasions.— *He hath not beheld Iniquity in* Jacob; *neither hath he seen Perverseness in* Israel (*d*).

P. You observe right; this Text has been sadly abused in support of that wretched Opinion; though it can have no manner of Relation to it.

It

(*a*) Ch. vii. 22, 23.
(*b*) *Quia etiamsi peccent, peccata illis neutiquam imputentur.*—St *Bernard* in *Septuag.* Serm. i.
(*c*) St Matth. vi. 23.
(*d*) Numb. xxiii. 21. It is worth any Scholar's while to see an excellent Dissertation on that Text by our learned *Gataker*; or an Extract of it in *Pool*'s *Synopsis.* The Meaning appears plainly to be,—God will not suffer his People to be *injuriously treated*, without taking *proper Notice* of it.

It appears most evidently plain, from the whole Dealings of God with that People, that he was so far from *not beholding*, or *not seeing* their Sins, that he made them frequently, *for their Sins*, a public Example of his righteous Displeasure. Let any one compare the divine Threatenings, in *Deuteronomy* xxviii. with what has befallen that unhappy Nation, and then consider, whether God did *not behold* Sin in his own People? That Relation they stood in to God, was so far from being a Licence to sin, or a Screen to protect them from Punishment, that, according to God's own Declaration, it exposed them the more certainly to it. Let us hear the Words of the Almighty himself,—*You only have I known of all the Families of the Earth: Therefore I will punish you for all your Iniquities* (*a*). One would hope, that no serious *Christian*, who duly laid these Things together, could ever imagine, that the *Sins of God's People or Children* were *not* entitled to Punishment, since it is for *this very Reason* that he threatens to punish them; because Sin in *them* was *more exceedingly sinful*; as being highly aggravated in every respect.

And here I must just take notice of another Text of Scripture, which has too often been mistaken and perverted. God Almighty, by his Prophet, tells the Wife of *Jeroboam*, that their Son *only shall come to the Grave, because*

___
(*a*) Amos iii. 2.

in him there is found [some] *good thing toward the Lord God of Israel* (a).

From hence very wicked Men may have sometimes received very great Encouragement; that is, in case *any thing good* was to be found in them. If here was any solid Foundation for Comfort, there are surely few so entirely abandoned, but might receive great Consolation from hence.

But then the Text really designs to give no such Comfort or Encouragement. It does not mean, that *though that Child was exceedingly wicked; yet as there was some good Disposition in him, therefore he was in the Favour of God*. It does not mean, that the *small good* in him made Amends for all the rest that was *bad*. And yet if this be not the Meaning, the weak Inference, drawn from this Passage, must fall to the Ground. Nay, it does not so much as intimate that there was *any Wickedness* in him at all. Our Translators having render'd the Passage — *some good Thing*, may have naturally led a mere *English* Reader into the Mistake; but it is amazing how Men of Learning could fall into it. The Word [*some*] is not in the Original; which, if literally translated, would run thus, — *there was found in him a good Word* (b) *towards the Lord*, &c. which, according to the *Hebrew* Idiom, might be rendered — there was

---

(a) 1 Kings xiv. 13.

(b) דבר טוב The Septuagint render it ῥῆμα καλὸν, and the Vulgate *Sermo bonus*.

was *Goodness* or a *good Intention* (a) in him towards God. The Father was a gross Idolater, whilst the Son seems to have been an Enemy to Idolatry, and a Worshipper of the true God. And therefore might design, when it was in his Power, to restore that *true Worship*, which his Father had corrupted, or rather had entirely overturned.

So that the Text only mentions the *Virtue* or *Piety* of the Youth; without the least Hint or Intimation that he lived in any wilful Sin or Offence against God. And therefore what Encouragement or Comfort can wicked Men receive from this Passage, though they may have *some* good Quality or other in them? It is melancholy and astonishing, that the sacred Oracles of God should be thus perverted, to the Ruin of Mankind! But it is an old Device of the great Enemy of Souls, to cause Men to *wrest* the Words of Life *to their own Destruction* (b).

E. I hope I shall always endeavour to remember those awful Words of the Holy Spirit,—*Whosoever shall keep the whole Law, and yet offend in one Point, he is guilty of all* (c). If these Words do not discover, that no *Christian* can safely indulge himself in *any one* Sin, I know not what can discover it.

P. You observe very right, my dear Friend. That single Sentence abundantly demon-

---

(a) The learned *Grotius* renders it, *Cogitatio bona, nam loqui Hebræis sæpe significat* Cogitare, in loc.

(b) 2 St Peter iii. 16.   (c) St James ii. 10

demonstrates that the *whole divine* Law must be kept. And that every wilful Violation of any Part of it, is an Affront offered to the Authority of God, whose Law it is; and that such Violation renders us liable to the Displeasure of that God, *who is of purer Eyes than to behold Evil*; and who *cannot look on Iniquity* (a) with Approbation.

E. I have still one Favour more to ask, and that is, to be informed, whether according to the Opinion of our Church, *Christians*, in these Days, may expect the *Inspiration* and *In-dwelling* of the Holy Spirit? Whether his *Influences* may be distinguished from the *natural* Operations of our own Minds? What his Illuminations may be? and whether he now ever *bears witness with our Spirit, that we are the Children of God?*

P. Let us in the first Place observe in general, what a thorough Sense our Church has of the Necessity of God's Holy Spirit.

And first, she declares in one of her Articles, that *Works done before the Grace of* Christ, *and the Inspiration of his Spirit, are not pleasant to God* (b). And therefore that all Orders and Degrees of Men may have this *Grace*, and this *Inspiration*, we pray, that the King may be *replenished with the Grace of* [God's] *Holy Spirit*; that the Royal Family may be *endued with the Holy Spirit*; and that the *healthful Spirit of* [Divine] *Grace* may be *sent down*

(a) Habak. i. 13.   (b) Article xiii.

down upon our *Bishops, and Curates, and all Congregations committed to their Charge* (*a*). That God would *cleanse the Thoughts of our Hearts by the Inspiration of his Holy Spirit* (*b*). And *inspire continually the universal Church with the Spirit of Truth* (*c*).

And though our Church be too wise to confound the *extraordinary* Gifts of the Spirit, such as *the Gift of Tongues, the Interpretation of Tongues, the Raising the Dead,* and such-like miraculous Powers, with those which belong to *Christians* in all Ages (*d*); yet we shall find that she supposes, and that with great Truth and Reason, that *Christians* receive *much more* from the Holy Spirit, than some Persons seem inclined to think or believe.

But in order to make this appear, we shall next take notice of what we meet with in the Collect for the Festival of St *Barnabas.*—" O Lord God Almighty, who didst en-
" dow thy holy Apostle *Barnabas* with sin-
" gular Gifts of the Holy Ghost, leave us
" not, we beseech thee, *destitute of thy mani-*
" *fold Gifts,* nor yet of Grace to use them al-
" way to thy Honour and Glory, *&c.*

We see here plainly, that in the Opinion of our Church, there are *manifold Gifts*
which

(*a*) See those Prayers.
(*b*) 1st Collect in the Communion Service.
(*c*) Prayer for the Church-Militant.
(*d*) 1 Cor xii. 9, 10, 29, 30. St Matth. xxviii. 20. St John xiv. 16, 17. Hom. for Whitsunday Part ii. p. 278, 279.

which belong to *Christians* of the prefent Times; fince fhe prays, that they may *not be left deftitute of them.* And in the Order of Confirmation, the Bifhop prays, that God would ftrengthen the Perfons to be confirmed, with the " Holy Ghoft; and daily in-
" creafe in them his manifold Gifts of Grace;
" the Spirit of Wifdom and Underftanding,
" the Spirit of Counfel and ghoftly Strength;
" the Spirit of Knowledge and true Godli-
" nefs; and that he would fill them with the
" Spirit of his holy Fear."

Farther he prays, " That they may daily
" increafe in God's Holy Spirit more and
" more; and be led in the Knowledge and
" Obedience of his Word."

But ftill to fee more clearly into our Church's Sentiments, with refpect to the Operations of the Holy Spirit, whether relating to the Heart and Affections, or to the Mind and Underftanding, let us take a View of the following Petitions,—*Grant us his Holy Spirit, that thofe Things may pleafe him which we do at this prefent; and that the reft of our Life hereafter may be pure and holy* (a).—*Take not thy holy Spirit from us* (b).—*The Fellowſhip of the Holy Ghoſt be with us all evermore* (c). —*Send to us thine Holy Ghoſt to comfort us* (d). *Grant that thy Holy Spirit may in all Things*
direct

(a) Abfolution.
(b) Refponfes after the Lord's Prayer.
(c) Conclufion of Morning and Evening Service.
(d) Sunday after Afcenfion.

direct and rule our Hearts (a).—*Grant that by thy holy Inspiration, we may think those Things that be good* (b). *Come, Holy Ghost, our Souls inspire; and lighten with celestial Fire* (c).

We may observe here, that in the Opinion of our Church, the Spirit of God is necessary to the *directing* our *Hearts*; to the *comforting* of our *Minds*; to the *thinking* what is good; to the *doing* what is *holy*; to the *enlightening* and *inspiring* our *Souls*; and to the *pleasing* of God. And this will yet still further appear. For, speaking of the *sanctifying* and *regenerating* Power of the Holy Ghost, she observes, that " The more it is hid from our Under-
" standing, the more it ought to move all
" Men to wonder at the secret and mighty
" working of God's Holy Spirit, which is
" *within us*. For it is the Holy Ghost, and
" no other Thing, that doth quicken the
" Minds of Men, stirring up good and godly
" Motions in their Hearts, which are agree-
" able to the Will and Commandment of
" God, such as otherwise of their own
" crooked and perverse Nature they should
" never have. *That which is born of the Spi-*
" *rit, is Spirit*, St John iii. 6. As who
" should say, Man of his own Nature is
" fleshly and carnal, corrupt and naught,
" sinful and disobedient to God, without any
" Spark of Goodness in him, without any
virtuous

(a) 19th after Trinity.
(b) 5th after Easter.   (c) *Veni Creator.*

" virtuous or godly Motion, only given to
" evil Thoughts and wicked Deeds. As for
" the Works of the Spirit, the Fruits of
" Faith, charitable and godly Motions, *if he*
" *have any at all in him*, they proceed *only* of
" the Holy Ghost, who is the only Worker
" of our *Sanctification*, and maketh us *new*
" *Men* in *Christ Jesus*.—Such is the Power
" of the Holy Ghost, to *regenerate Men*, and
" as it were to bring them forth *anew*, so
" that they shall be nothing like the Men
" they were before. Neither doth he think
" it sufficient inwardly to work the *spiritual*
" *and new Birth* of Man, unless he do also
" *dwell* and *abide in* him.—O what Comfort
" is this to the Heart of a true *Christian*, to
" think that the Holy Ghost *dwelleth within*
" *him* (*a*)!"

 Again, " Thou hast received [the Body of
" *Christ*] to have *within* thee, the Father, the
" Son, and the Holy Ghost, for to *dwell*
" *with thee*, to endow thee with Grace, to
" strengthen thee against thine Enemies, and
" to comfort thee with their *Presence* (*b*).—
" A true *Christian* is the Temple of the Ho-
" ly Ghost (*c*)."

 As these Passages sufficiently discover what
our Church thinks of the *In-dwelling* of the
Spirit; so they abundantly shew, that she supposes the *Operations* of that Holy Spirit are
very

(*a*) Homily for Whitsunday, Part I. p. 276, 277.
(*b*) Hom. of the Resurrection, p. 262.
(*c*) Hom. against the Fear of Death, Part i. p. 52.

very easy to be distinguished from the *natural Workings* of our own Minds. For if it be really true, that every *good* Thought and Disposition proceed from the Spirit of God (*a*); and every thing *bad* from a *corrupt* Heart, and a wicked *Tempter* (*b*); it can be no difficult matter to ascribe Good and Evil to their proper Authors. If our Hearts are renewed and sanctified, and produce the Fruits of the Gospel; yet *all this* is the Work of the Holy Spirit, and to him let the Honour be given. —And as to his *dwelling* in us; miserable is the Case of that Person, where he *dwells* not. —For *if any Man have not the Spirit of* Christ, *he is none of his.* But *if the Spirit of him that raised up* Jesus *from the Dead, dwell in you; he that raised up* Christ *from the Dead, shall also quicken your mortal Bodies, by his Spirit that dwelleth in you* (*c*). —*Know ye not that ye are the Temple of God; and that the Spirit of God dwelleth in you* (*d*)?—And the same Apostle tells the *Ephesians*, that they *were built together for an Habitation of God through the Spirit.* And gives them this strict Caution— *not to grieve the Holy Spirit of God, whereby they were sealed unto the Day of Redemption* (*e*). So that, I presume, our Church's Opinion, both as to the *Difference* between the natural
Workings

(*a*) Gal. v. 22, 23.
(*b*) St Matth. xv. 19. Gal. v. 19—21. Ephes. vi. 11, 12. 1 Thess. iii. 5. 2 Cor xi. 3.
(*c*) Rom. viii. 9—11.
(*d*) 1 Cor. iii. 16. . (*e*) Ephes. ii. 22. Ch. iv. 30.

Workings of *corrupt Nature*, and the Operations of the *Holy Ghost*; as well as to the *Dwelling* of that divine Spirit within us, is well founded; as having the sacred Oracles entirely on her Side.

But let us still further hear her Opinion.—In the 17th Article she mentions "such Per-"sons as *feel* in themselves the Working of "the Spirit of *Christ*, drawing up their Mind "to high and heavenly Things."

Again, every *Deacon*, at his Ordination, is thus examined—"Do you trust that you "are inwardly moved by the Holy Ghost, "to take upon you this Office and Mini-"stration (*a*)?" And when they come to be ordained *Priests*, the *Bishop* acquaints them that they *ought, and have need to pray earnestly for God's Holy Spirit*. And afterwards, they are admonished,——*continually to pray for the heavenly Assistance of the Holy Ghost* (*b*). Towards the Conclusion of the Service, the Bishop lays his Hands on the Head of every one; pronouncing these solemn Words,—*Receive the Holy Ghost for the Office and Work of a Priest in the Church of God*, &c.

Again, in one of the *Homilies*, after it has been observed, that *all Spiritual Gifts come from God by* Jesus Christ, we read as follows, ——" God give us Grace——to *know* these "Things, and to *feel* them in our Hearts.
" This

(*a*) See the Office for ordaining *Deacons*.
(*b*) Exhortation in the Office for ordaining *Priests*.

" This *Knowledge* and *Feeling* are not in
" ourselves ;—Let us therefore meekly call
" upon—the Holy Ghost,—that he would
" assist us, and *inspire* us with his Pre-
" sence, *&c.*"

And moreover in the same Homily it is declared, that " It is by this Holy Spirit,
" which maketh Intercession for us, with
" continual Sighs, that we may boldly come
" in Prayer, and call upon Almighty God,
" as *our* Father (*a*)." *Rom.* viii. 15, 26. *Gal.* iv. 6.

But now surely, if, through the Holy Spirit, we are enabled to approach God as *our* Father, it must appear a sufficient Evidence that we are *His* Children. The one very plainly follows from the other.

If we are assisted by the Spirit to call God *our* Father; it is so far *bearing Witness*, that *we are the Children of God*. This the great Apostle affirms to be the State of the *Christians* in those Days (*b*); and what, but our own Corruptions, can be the Reason, why that Holy Spirit will no longer *bear* [the same] *Witness* with *our* Spirit? *He that believeth on the Son of God*, says the beloved Disciple, *has the Witness in himself* (*c*). But what *Witness* is this, which the *Believer* has *in himself?* No other surely, but the *Witness* of the Holy Ghost.

The late learned Dr *Whitby*, who was far from

(*a*) Homily for Rogation Week, Part iii. p. 293, 294.
(*b*) Rom. viii. 16.   (*c*) 1 St John v. 10.

from being an *Enthusiastic* Commentator, thus interprets those Words,—*As having in himself that Spirit of God which gives this Testimony to* Christ (a). 'Tis true the Testimony here given relates to *Christ*; but still it is given by the Holy Spirit: And this Holy Spirit is *in* the *Believer*. Undoubtedly the *Witness* of the *Spirit* that Men *are the Children of God*, can belong only to *those*, who are his *real Children*; as the learned *Grotius* observes (b): But why it should not be the Privilege of *all such*, in *all* Ages of *Christianity*, remains to be proved. If that *Holy Spirit will make his Abode in the Minds of true* Christians, *even to the Time of their Resurrection*, as the same great Man affirms (c); or, as is sufficiently intimated by a much greater, even the inspired Apostle St *Paul* (d); can we suppose he will there abide, without ever giving the same Testimony to the *Children of God*, which he formerly did?—I know it may be said, that the Church then enjoyed many great Privileges and Powers which we enjoy not. However, as the *Power*, or *Right*, or *Privilege of becoming the Sons of God*, belongs now *to as many as truly receive* Christ *by Faith*, and are

---

(a) In Loc.

(b) *Deus tale donum non dat nisi iis quos pro Filiis habere vult.*—in Rom. viii. 16.

(c) *Spiritus ille Sanctus in Animis Christianorum habitans, &, si solicitè servetur, ad Mortem, imò & post Mortem ad Resurrectionem usque, Animis adhærens.*—in 1 Thess. v. 23.   (d) Rom. viii. 11.

are born of God (a); as *all are now the Children of God by Faith in* Christ Jesus (b); so is it surely of Consequence *now* to know, whether *Christians* are, in Truth and Reality, *Children of God*; *Heirs of God*; *and Joint-heirs with* Christ (c).

This appears to be of the same Importance, in every Age and State of the Church.

E. But may it not be said, that there can be no Occasion for the Holy Spirit thus to *bear Witness*; since the Apostle has laid down other Marks, by which to judge, whether we are the *Children of God*, or not: Such as *mortifying the Deeds of the Body through the Spirit*: And assuring us, that *as many as are led by the Spirit of God, they are the Sons of God* (d).

P. It is undoubtedly a most infallible Proof, we are not *the Sons of God*, if we are not *led by his Spirit*; and do not, *through him, mortify the Deeds of the Body*.

But will it follow from hence, that God has never given any other way of discovering that Mankind *are his Chidren?* For if there be any Force in this Argument, it will conclude as well against the first Times, as the present. Or shall Men pretend to limit those Ways; or settle the Number of them? Let us only observe what immediately follows the two Verses you just mentioned.—*For ye have not received the Spirit of*

(a) St John i. 12, 13.   (b) Gal. iii. 26.
(c) Rom. viii. 17.   (d) Rom. viii. 13, 14.

of Bondage again to fear; but ye have received the Spirit of Adoption, whereby we cry, Abba, Father. *The Spirit itself beareth Witness with our Spirit, that we are the Children of God* (a).

As if the Apostle had said,——" That " Spirit of God, through whom ye must " *mortify the Deeds of the Body*; and by " whom you must be *led*, if you desire " *to be the Sons of God*; that Spirit of God " is he, whom you have already received, " to convince you of your Sin and Dan-" ger, and to deliver you from the *Bondage* " *of Corruption*, the Dominion of Sin and " Satan, and the Fear of Death, *into the* " *glorious Liberty of the Children of God:* " And he is therefore now to us, the *Spi-" rit of Adoption*; by whom we are en-" abled to call God *our* Father. He it is " that now *bears Witness* within us, or joint-" ly *with our Spirit*, that *we are the Children* " *of God* (b)."

This

(a) Verse 15, 16.

(b) I humbly apprehend, that by this the Apostle means, some *divine Operation* of the *Holy Spirit* upon the Soul; by which we receive a *clear* and *joyful* Assurance, that we are the *Children of God*. For the *inward Kingdom of God* is not only *Righteousness*, but *Peace* and *Joy* in the *Holy Ghost*, Rom. xiv. 17. Ch. v. 1. Ch. xv. 13. —Therefore it is humbly submitted,—Whether " *the* " *Spirit itself bearing Witness with our Spirit, that we* " *are the Children of God*,"— does not seem plainly to include something more than merely *Inclination* and *Power* to obey the divine Commands? Undoubtedly, if either

This seems in general to be the plain Meaning and Design of the Apostle; though some have endeavoured, with great Industry, to explain this obvious Meaning away; by supposing it referr'd only to the *working of Miracles*.

I will here just further observe, that our Church, speaking of the ancient Patriarchs mentioned by St *Paul*, [Heb. xi.] thus remarks—" by the coming of our Saviour " *Christ*, we have received *more abundant-* " *ly* the Spirit of God in our Hearts, " whereby we may receive *a greater Faith*, " and a *surer Trust* than many of them " had (*a*)."

But let us next proceed to consider, how far our Church supposes the Holy Spirit may enlighten our Minds or Understandings. And either *Inclination*, or *Will*, or *Power*, be wanting, I should not scruple to tell the most *sanguine Believer*, that all his *Joy*, and *Peace*, and *Assurance*, were only so many Delusions.—But yet, when we read of *a full Assurance of Faith and Hope*; of receiving the *Spirit of Adoption*; of his *witnessing with our Spirit, that we are the Children of God*; and of being *filled with all Joy and Peace in believing*;—I can make no doubt, but that *inward Witness of the Spirit* is sometimes attended with a *Strength* and *Clearness of Evidence*, that cannot be resisted; and with a *Joy* and *Peace*, that cannot be described. But tho' the *Spirit* works differently in different Persons, just as infinite Wisdom sees proper: yet, I presume, that " *his* " *bearing Witness with our Spirit, that we are the Children* " *of God*."—always implies a sufficient Degree of *Evidence*, immediately communicated to the Soul, and attended with much *Joy and Peace in believing*.

(*a*) Hom. of Faith, Part ii. p. 22.

And firſt, ſhe approves of theſe Sayings of St *Chryſoſtom*, where he thus expreſſes himſelf, with regard to the finding out the Senſe of the *Holy Scripture*.—" God himſelf from
" above, will give *Light unto our Minds*, and
" *teach* us thoſe Things which are neceſſary
" for us, and wherein we be ignorant."—

" Man's human or worldly Wiſdom, or
" Science, is not needful to the underſtand-
" ing of Scripture, but the *Revelation* of
" the Holy Ghoſt, who *inſpireth* the true
" Meaning unto them, that with Humili-
" ty and Diligence do ſearch therefore *(a)*."
—At the Ordination of a Prieſt, the Biſhop, thus prays,—" *That we may* daily increaſe
" and go forwards in the *Knowledge* and
" *Faith* of thee and thy Son, *by the Holy*
" *Spirit*."

Again, our Church, ſpeaking of divine Wiſdom, obſerves that *This Wiſdom cannot be attained, but by the Direction of the Spirit of God* (b).—*This Holy Spirit will ſuggeſt unto us that* [which] *ſhall be wholeſome, and confirm us in all Things* (c).

And therefore it is no Wonder, that our Church thus addreſſes herſelf to God—*Grant us, by the ſame Spirit, to have a right Judgment in all Things* (d).

Moreover,

(*a*) Hom. of the Holy Scripture, Part. ii. p 5.
(*b*) Hom. for Rogation-Week, Part iii. p. 294.
(*c*) P. 297.   (*d*) Collect for Whitſunday.

Moreover, at the Confecration of every Bifhop, and at the Ordination of a Prieft, thefe Words are repeated,—

Enable with perpetual Light
The Dulnefs of our blinded Sight.

Or elfe the following,

O Holy Ghoft, into our Minds
Send down thy heavenly Light (a).

And further, at the Confecration of a Bifhop, the Archbifhop enquires of the Bifhop elect,—*Whether he will faithfully exercife himfelf in the Holy Scriptures, and call upon God by Prayer for the true underftanding of the fame* (b)?

But muft not this *true underftanding* arife from the Holy Spirit? And whether we call fuch Affiftance of the Spirit, by the Name of *Influence, Direction, Illumination, Suggeftion,* or *Infpiration*; where is the Difference? Some Operation of the Holy Spirit, it certainly muft be: Though *how,* or in *what Way,* or *Manner,* that divine Spirit fhall fee proper to operate, cannot render it lefs a *divine Operation.*

But laftly, the Archbifhop prays, that *God would fo endue* [the Bifhop] *with his Holy Spirit, that he preaching the Word* [of God] *may be earneft to reprove, befeech, and rebuke,*

(a) *Veni Creator.* See the Confecration and Ordination Service.

(b) **Confecration of Bifhops.**

buke,—*and also may be a wholesome Example to Believers* (a).

So that the Holy Spirit is here evidently prayed for, not only that the Bishop may be a *Pattern* to others; but also that he may be enabled to *instruct* both by *earnest Reproof* and *Exhortation.*

All which plainly imply not only the *sanctifying* Influences of the Holy Ghost; but also *spiritual Strength, Courage,* and *Resolution,—constantly to speak the Truth; boldly to rebuke Vice; and patiently to suffer for the Truth's sake,* as our Church elsewhere expresses herself (b). For though these three last Petitions are not there particularly applied to *one Order* of Pastors more than another; yet they must in a very eminent Degree belong to those of the *higher* Order; as being, by their great Superiority of Station, most capable of doing an Honour to Religion. They are, in a very peculiar Manner, what our blessed Lord calls—*the Light of the World;* and *a City that is set on an Hill* (c). Consequently a *diligent preaching* the *Holy Word* of God (d); a resolute and *bold rebuking of Vice,* in all Orders and Degrees of Men whatever; an earnest reproving of Sinners, without *Favour, Fear,* or *Affection;* a *painful,* and *constant* enforcing the *Truths of the Gospel;* and the *patiently* bearing any Reproach,

(a) Second Prayer before the Benediction.
(b) Collect for St John Baptist's Day.
(c) St Matth. v. 14.   (d) Collect for St Peter's.

proach, Contempt, or Perfecution for the *Sake of thofe divine Truths*; all thefe muſt prove of greater Weight and Influence from ſuch, than the fame Behaviour in obſcurer Perſons. And therefore it is highly neceſſary, in order to anſwer theſe great Purpoſes, that they ſhould be *endued*, in a very ſingular manner, *with God's Holy Spirit*. That ſo by the Exemplarineſs of their Lives and Behaviour, and the Soundneſs of their Inſtructions, *their Light may ſo ſhine before Men, that they may ſee their good Works, and glorify their Father, which is in Heaven* (a). And thus our Church expreſsly prays in the following Words,—" Give Grace, O heavenly " Father, to all Biſhops and Curates, that " they may both by their *Life* and *Doctrine* " ſet forth thy true and lively Word, and " rightly and duly adminiſter thy Holy Sa- " craments (b)."

Here the *Grace* or *Aſſiſtance* of the Holy Spirit is requeſted, that both the *ſuperior* and *inferior* Paſtors may ſo *live*, and ſo *inſtruct*, as may beſt promote the Truths of God's divine Word; and that they might likewiſe adminiſter his Holy Sacraments in a ſuitable and becoming manner. And this again, with ſome further Addition, is petitioned for in that excellent Prayer, called the *Litany*.— " That it may pleaſe thee to *illuminate* all " Biſhops, Prieſts, and Deacons, with *true* " Know-

(a) St Matth. v. 16.
(b) Prayer for the Church Militant.

" *Knowledge* and *Understanding* of thy Word,
" and that both by their Preaching and Liv-
" ing they may set it forth, and shew it ac-
" cordingly."

Here we beseech *the Father of Lights* to *illuminate* or enlighten all the three Orders of our Church with *divine Knowledge and Understanding*; and that, according to the Measure bestowed on them, they may, both by their *Preaching and Living*, set forth and declare the sacred Word of God. All which very manifestly proves, that, in the Opinion of our Church, the *Illumination* of the Spirit of God is necessary to their *true Knowledge and Understanding* of his divine Word; and for the enforcing of it, both by their *Lives* and *Doctrines*.

And thus have I endeavoured to satisfy your Enquiries, concerning our Church's Opinion, with regard to the *present Operations* or Influences of the Holy Spirit*.

E. It appears indeed pretty plain, what our Church thinks of these Things. But I have often heard a great Difference made between *immediate* Inspiration, and an *Inspiration* or *Influence* which is *not* immediate.

P. What-

* If *such Operations* of the *Holy Spirit* have a plain Foundation in the *Gospel*, how melancholy is the Reflection, that the *looking for them* should be called by the learned Bishop of *Gloucester*, " *superstitious* and *fanatical!*" *Essay on Grace.*—May that *illuminating Spirit* instruct him *better!*

P. Whatever Difference there may be in the Manner of the Holy Spirit's displaying his Power; yet surely, if a Person's Mind be *enlightened,* or his Heart *cleansed* by this divine Spirit;—whether these Effects are produced by an *immediate* Influence, or by the Interposition of some Means or Instrument; yet the Effects are still equally owing to the *Spirit of God.*

When our blessed Lord applied *Clay* to the Eyes of the Blind, before he restored his Sight; was that Miracle the less owing to his *divine Power?* Or was not here altogether the *same divine Power* that cured the *Leper,* only with saying,——*I will, be thou clean?*

If it should be objected, that there is a wide Difference between making use of Means that can have no Tendency to cure, or which are rather opposite to it; and making use of Means that seem to *co-operate*; and which only want a Blessing to attend them: If this should be objected, it must be owned, that there is undoubtedly a great deal of Difference in the Nature of *Means.* But then, where the most *promising* Means will *not do,* without the *Assistance* of the Holy Spirit: nay, where the *self-same* Means will *always* succeed *with him,* but never *without* him, there surely the *whole* is to be ascribed to *him.*

The same divine Word, for Instance, proved a *Savour of Life unto Life* to some; but a *Savour of Death unto Death* to others (*a*).

The *Preaching of* Christ *crucified* was to the *Jews a Stumbling-block*; and to the *Greeks, Foolishness:* But to many, it proved *the Power of God, and the Wisdom of God* (*b*). Here was the *same divine Word* of the *same divine Spirit*; and yet it proved, for Want of his divine Power upon the Soul, of no Force or Efficacy with regard to Numbers. His efficacious Influence was wanting, which those Persons were not fit to receive. And indeed without such Influence, the divine Word will prove but a *dead Letter* to us, and leave us in the *Gall of Bitterness, and Bond of Iniquity.* This is the true Reason, why some may often *hear* and *read* the Gospel, without *believing* one Word of it. And this is the Reason, why so many others, who call themselves *Believers*, are not one whit the better for *all their Belief.* This discovers the absolute Necessity of the Holy Spirit's constant Assistance —— Though whether *mediate* or *immediate*, should be left to him, who knows best in what *Manner* and *Measure* to work in us

The great Apostle, who had undoubtedly instructed the *Ephesians*, what was the *Hope of God's Calling*, and what the *Riches of the Glory of his Inheritance in the Saints*; and what the *exceeding Greatness of his Power*; yet prays that the *Eyes of their Understanding may*

(*a*) 2 Cor. ii. 15, 16.   (*b*) 1 Cor. i. 23, 24.

may be enlightened in order to *know* these Things (*a*): And exhorts them to be *filled with the Spirit* (*b*). And surely, if *divine Illumination* was wanted after *such* an *Instructor*; can any wise and serious *Christian* think the same *Illumination* to be now *needless?* But whatever may be supposed by some, it is evident our Church thinks more wisely.

However, if Men will but allow, that the *Assistance* of the Holy Spirit is altogether necessary to the *opening* and *instructing* of the Mind; to the *softening* and *purifying* the Heart; and to the carrying us through the great Work of Salvation, never dispute with them about the *Form* of their Expressions.

E. As I am sensible of my Obligations for this Trouble; so am I sensible that my great Business is, to obtain this divine Assistance for conducting me safe through this World, *to the Regions of everlasting Happiness.*

P. That, my dear Friend, is undoubtedly the main and principal Business of every one. And therefore I shall just add a few short Cautions and Directions, which may prove of some further Service to you. And now, if you do but thoroughly consider the true Nature of the Gospel of *Christ*, you will certainly conclude, that all those various Ways, which Men have taken to break the Force of its divine Precepts and Doctrines,

---

(*a*) Ephes. i. 17—19. See Acts xx. 17—21.
(*b*) Ephes. v. 18.

trines, are only so many various Delusions of the Devil.—Some, for Instance, have imagined, that certain of its Precepts are not binding in themselves; but are only what *may*, or may *not* be complied with, just according to our own Choice and Liking. These, by the Church of *Rome*, are called *Counsels* of *Perfection*.—See Bishop *Burnet* on *Article* xiv.

Others have talked of a *secret* Will in God, which differs from that which is *revealed*. And which Opinion directly sets aside the whole Authority of *divine Revelation*. For it is only supposing that what I do not approve of in Revelation, is contrary to the *secret* Will of God; and then the whole Force of his *revealed* Will is lost upon me. It is much the same thing, and must have just the same Effects, with supposing some Doctrines in the *sacred Writings* are of divine Authority; whilst others have only been foisted in by ignorant and designing Men. For what Weight can the *Holy Scriptures* have with us, whilst we are under the Influence of such a Delusion? We shall infallibly ascribe every thing, which we do not like, to the *Mistakes* of some, or the *Craft* of others: And consequently the whole Force of such Doctrines, or Precepts, will vanish into Air.— Be assured, God has taken more Care of his divine Word, than some Men apprehend. However, I would not be misunderstood; I do not mean to say, that there are

no

no various Readings in the sacred Oracles; for there are many thousands in the *New Testament*. But then, when it is considered, that none of these *Variations* make the least material Difference either as to the *Faith* or *Practice* of a *Christian*, the Greatness of the Number is only a stronger Confirmation, God has taken even a *miraculous Care* of his own sacred Truths.

A late learned Writer, speaking of these various *Lections*, thus expresses himself,—" *Nor is one Article of Faith or moral Pre-*" *cept either perverted or lost in them*; *choose* " *as aukwardly as you can, choose the worst* " *by Design, out of the whole Lump of Read-*" *ings* (a)."

But again, some have thought that the stricter Precepts of the Gospel (those particularly contained in our Lord's divine Sermon on the Mount) related *only* to the *Apostles*; though nothing is more evident, than that our blessed Lord delivered these divine Doctrines to the *People*, as well as to *them*: For we read, that *the People were astonished at his Doctrine* (b).

Others have gone a Step farther, and supposed that the whole Gospel must abate of its original Strictness; as being far too high for the Attainment of Mankind. So that

since

(a) Remarks upon Freethinking, by *Phileleutherus Lipsiensis*. Part I. Sect. 32.

(b) St Matth. vii. 28. See the learned *Grotius* and *Hammond* on St Matth. v. 1.

since we are not able to reach up to that; it must therefore itself come down to us. —As these *Persons* seem only to have an Eye at their *own Strength* and *Abilities*, it is no wonder they despair of Success. But let such remember, that a Power superior to their own, is ready to make them *more than Conquerors:* And that it is their own Fault, if they cannot *do all Things through* Christ *that strengthens them* (*a*). The Holy Spirit never amuses Men with vain Shadows; nor proposes *stricter* Duties, than he is both *able,* and *willing* to assist us in performing.

If any Man will come after me, says the Son of God, *let him deny himself, and take up his Cross daily, and follow me* (*b*). To the same Purpose spake our blessed Lord to the *Multitude*, as well as to his own *Disciples* (*c*).

No doubt, this appeared a very *hard Saying* to many; but it was not the less true, even in the *strictest* Sense of the Words. But if we should fancy ourselves not much concerned in this *harsh* Sentence, in these Days of *Plenty*, and *Ease*, and *Prosperity*, we shall find that we are unhappily mistaken. For though we should not *suffer Persecution* for resolving to *live godly* in *Christ Jesus* (*d*): for *not being conformed to this World*;

(*a*) Rom. viii. 35—39. Philip. iv. 13.
(*b*) St Luke ix. 23.
(*c*) St Mark viii. 34. St Luke xiv. 25—27, 33.
(*d*) 2 Tim. iii. 12.

World; to the Vices, Follies, and Vanities of a wretched, thoughtless Age:—Though we should not be exposed to any kind of ill Treatment, for labouring to *be transformed by the renewing of our Mind* (a); for *setting our Affections on Things above* (b); and having *our Conversation in Heaven* (c); yet every wise *Christian* must know, that there is abundant room for *daily* obeying this Command of *Christ*, even in the midst of the greatest *Plenty, Ease*, and *Prosperity*.

It is indeed greatly to be feared, that *all* do not think of *daily denying themselves* in such Circumstances, and *of taking up their Cross*, and following *Christ*; but still his divine Command is in full Force: And they who reject it, are neither *his Disciples*, nor *worthy of him* (d).—In short, if Mankind would but part with their Pride, their Luxury, their Wrath, their Covetousness, their vicious Hearts, and worldly Minds, they would never imagine that the Gospel of *Christ* was too *strict*, or too *severe*.

But again, some others have gone so surprising a length, as not only to affirm, but even to attempt to prove it, from the Gospel itself,—that *all shall be saved, let them live as they will!*—If such Writers are serious, as may be much questioned, their Minds must be too much distempered to be capable of

(a) Rom. xii. 2. (b) Col. iii. 1, 2.
(c) Phil. iii. 20.
(d) St Luke xiv. 27. St Math. x. 38.

of being reasoned with. But if they are acting only the Part of *Buffoons*, I pray God they may see their Wickedness, before it be too late.

All these Notions, and others of a like nature, may be esteemed more or less as the *Depths of Satan*, to beguile unwary Souls; to tempt them from the Simplicity of the Gospel; and to carry them from one degree of Folly and Infatuation to another. These Notions, my dear Friend, are not *the Truth as it is in* Jesus.

You, and I, and every *Christian*, are called to high and glorious Privileges.

Even to *abide in Christ*; and *Christ in us* (*a*). To *put on the Lord* Jesus Christ (*b*). To *glory in the Cross of our Lord* Jesus Christ; to be *crucified unto the World*; and to have *the World crucified unto us*. To have *Christ formed in us*; and *dwelling in our Hearts by Faith*. And *the Life which we live in the Flesh, to live by the Faith of the Son of God* (*c*).

In a word, To have *our Conversation in Heaven*; to be *an Habitation of God through the*

(*a*) St John xv. 4, 5.

(*b*) Rom. iii. 14. Gal. iii. 27. εἰ γὰρ Χριστὸν τὸν υἱὸν τοῦ Θεοῦ ἐνδεδύμεθα, καὶ πρὸς αὐτὸν ἐφωμοιώθημεν. εἰς μίαν συγγένειαν κ᾽ μίαν ἰδέαν ἤχθημεν, χάριτι γεγονότες ὅπερ ἐκεῖνός ἐστι φύσει Theoph. in Gal. iii. 27.

Christum induunt verè Christiani quique a Deo sibi, tum 1, *imputantum, ad justificationem*; *tum* 2, *impertitum, ad sanctificationem.*—Gatak. Cinni. cap. ix. p. 101, 102.

(*c*) Gal. vi. 14. Ch. iv. 19. Ephes. iii. 17. Gal. ii. 20.

the *Spirit*; to be *filled with all the Fulness of God:* And to be made *Partakers of the divine Nature* (*a*).

Thus, in the Language of our own Church, are we to *dwell in* Christ, *and* Christ *in us*; *We are* to be *One with* Christ, *and* Christ *with us* (*b*). And moreover we pray, *that we may evermore dwell in him, and he in us* (*c*).

And surely sufficient Reason is there thus perpetually to pray; since our blessed Lord has himself assured us, that *without him* [if *separated* from him] *we can do nothing* (*d*). As our holy Lord had been just comparing the Union betwixt himself and his Disciples, to the *Vital Union* betwixt a *Vine* and its *Branches*; it is evident he here speaks of such a Separation from himself (*e*), as cuts off all spiritual Communications to the Soul, and leaves us destitute of all divine Life. So deplorable is the State of being *without Christ!*—Undoubtedly, my dear Friend, the *Religion* of the Gospel is a very great Work; and *there are many Adversaries*. But let every true *Christian* take Courage; for *greater is he that is in them, than he that is in the*

(*a*) Philip. iii. 20. Ephes. ii. 22. Ch. iii. 19. 2 St Peter i. 4. See also 1 St John ii. 20, 24. Ch. iii. 24. Ch. iv. 13, 15. Ch. v. 20.

(*b*) Exhortation in the Communion-Service.

(*c*) Prayer before the Prayer of Consecration.

(*d*) St John xv. 5.

(*e*) χωρὶς ἐμοῦ. i. e. χωρισθέντες ἀπ' ἐμοῦ, *separati à me.* Piscator in Loc.

the World (*a*). And happy is it, that he is so; since *Christians* are so thickly beset with Enemies. They must not only look for Insults, Reproach, and Contempt, from a vain bad World; but may expect that even their own *irregular Appetites* and *Passions* will enter into a formal Controversy, and go near to demand,—*What they were given for?*— To which, I think, you may well reply, that with regard to the State they are in, —*they were not given by God at all.*

God created nothing *irregular*. All that he made, was *good*. God *created Man in his own Image, and after his own Likeness. He made Man upright; but they have sought out many Inventions* (*b*). All their *Irregularities* are therefore owing to a subtil Tempter; to corrupt Nature, and to Mens indulging of it. But as it was the great Design of *Christ*'s coming into the World to *restore* that *divine Life* which we had lost; to *renew us in the Spirit of our Mind*; to bestow on us that *new Man, which after God is created in Righteousness and true Holiness;—which is renewed in Knowledge, after the Image of him that created him* (*c*); Therefore all *irregular Desires*, all *inordinate Affections* (as being opposite to these great Ends) must not only be restrained and bridled,

---

(*a*) 1 St John iv. 4.
(*b*) Gen. i. 26, 27, 31. Eccles. vii. 29.
(*c*) Rom. vi. 23. 1 Cor. xv. 22. 2 Cor. v. 18, 19. Ephes. iv. 22—24. Col. iii. 10.

bridled, but also entirely subdued and *mortified* (*a*).

And now, as the *sacred Oracles* contain the *Mystery of God and of* Christ; *in whom are hid all the Treasures of Wisdom and Knowledge* (*b*); let me advise you frequently to meditate on the divine Truths which are therein contained. Be assured, you will never repent of the Time thus laid out. Do not be afraid of being over-lavish of your Pains and Labour in such a Study, since it will bring its own Reward along with it.

And here I must mention a few Lines from that very learned Prelate, the late excellent Bishop *Stillingfleet*, where he treats of the *divine Authority* of the *Scriptures*.—
" How dry and sapless are all the volumi-
" nous Discourses of *Philosophers*, compared
" with this *Sentence*,—Jesus Christ *came in-*
" *to the World to save Sinners!* 1 Tim. i. 15.
" How *jejune* and *unsatisfactory* are all the
" *Discoveries* they had of *God* and his
" *Goodness*, in Comparison of what we
" have by the *Gospel* of *Christ!* Well might
" *Paul* then say,—*That he determined to*
" *know nothing but* Christ, *and him crucifi-*
" *ed*, 1 Cor. ii. 2. *Christ crucified* is the *Li-*
" brary which *Triumphant Souls* will be *stu-*
" *dying* in to all *Eternity*. This is the on-
" ly *Library*, which is the true ἰατρεῖον ψυχῆς,
" that which *cures* the *Soul* of all its *Ma-*
" *ladies*

" *ladies* and *Diſtempers*. Other Knowledge
" makes Mens Minds *giddy* and *flatulent*;
" this *ſettles* and *compoſes* them. Other
" Knowledge is apt to *ſwell* Men into high
" *Conceits* and *Opinions* of themſelves; this
" brings them to the trueſt *View* of them-
" ſelves; and thereby to *Humility* and *So-*
" *briety*. Other Knowledge *leaves* Mens
" Hearts as it found them; this *alters* them,
" and *makes* them better. So tranſcendent
" an *Excellency* is there in the *Knowledge*
" of *Chriſt crucified*, above the ſublimeſt Spe-
" culations in the World (*a*)."

All theſe beautiful Obſervations, I am certain, you will find true, by your own happy Experience. But then, as *Humility* of *Mind*, and *Holineſs* of Heart, are the beſt *Key* to the Goſpel of *Chriſt* (*b*), next to *divine Illumination*; therefore I beſeech you to petition conſtantly for an *humble* and *ſanctified* Spirit: Since theſe will go a great way towards clearing up of many Difficulties. Our Church ſays, that " he profits moſt in read-
" ing the Word of God, that is moſt *turn-*
" *ed* into it; that is moſt *inſpired* with the
" Holy Ghoſt; [who is] moſt in his Heart
" and Life altered and changed into that
" Thing which he readeth: He that is dai-
" ly leſs and leſs *proud*, leſs *wrathful*, leſs
" *covetous*, and leſs deſirous of *worldly* and
" vain

(*a*) *Origines Sacræ*, l. iii. c. vi. p. 256. Edit. 5.
(*b*) St Matth. v. 8. St John v. 44. Ch. vii. 17. St James i. 5. Ch. iv. 6. 1 St Pet. v. 5.

" *vain Pleasures*: He that *daily* (forsaking his old vicious Life) increaseth in Virtue more and more (*a*)."

And now, may every Professor of *Christianity* sincerely pray to be thus qualified, for the Sake of the *Great Author and Finisher of our Faith*.

E. And may I, in particular, my dear Friend, reap the Benefit of your kind Advice and Instructions.

P. I pray God succeed them, my good Friend, *Eugenius*.

(*a*) Hom. of the Reading and Knowledge of the Holy Scripture, Part I. p. 3.

APPENDIX.

APPENDIX.

HAVING very lately met with a *Book*, wrote by a learned Gentleman, in which are some few things very different, in my humble Opinion, from the *Doctrine* of the *Gospel*; I chose, by way of *Appendix*, to take some Notice of them in this separate Manner, rather than to disperse the *Remarks* through various Parts of the *Dialogues*.

It was not judged *material* to mention the *Author's* Name, as the Reader is only desired to consider the *Arguments*, which are here offered.

But first, let us attend to that glorious Description of *Divine Faith*, which the *Sacred Oracles* have given us.

" *Faith* is the Substance of Things hoped
" for; the Evidence of Things not seen.
" It is a Principle of the *Operation of God*;
" which *purifies the Heart*; and gains the
" *Victory* over the World; [its Terrors, Allurements and Temptations] " It works by
" Love; is the *Breast-plate of Righteousness*;
" and a *Shield*, which can *quench all the fiery*
" *Darts of the Devil* (a)."

Here

(a) Heb. xi. 1. Col. ii. 12. Acts xv. 9. Ch. xxvi. 18. 1 St John v. 4. Gal. v. 6. 1 Thess. v. 8. Ephes. vi. 14, 16. τῦ πονηρῦ.

Here then is a *divine living Principle*, sufficient to stir up every *Faculty* of the *Soul*; and to *inspire* us with *Courage* and *Resolution* to trample the *World*, and the *God of it*, under our Feet.

Let this be now compared with the Description given of *Faith* by the *ingenious Writer* just mentioned.

" *Faith signifies the believing the Word of*
" *God; assenting to it; relying*, or *resting*
" *upon it; and acting accordingly*."

Can it be any wonder, that *such a Faith* should leave Men *in Sin*; and that " *Death*
" *must be sent at last to kill it*;" and thus give the *Believer* a final Deliverance? For surely the *Faith* here described can never make *Felix*, nor the *Jailor, tremble*. It can never, by any *Virtue* of its own, cause one Soul to cry out,——*What must I do to be saved?* Nor can it, by any *intrinsic Power* in itself, *gain the Victory over the World, the Flesh, or the Devil*. For do not we see Multitudes of *warm Professors*, who *believe, assent, rely*, and *rest, upon the Word of God*;—and yet continue all their Lives *in the Gall of Bitterness, and Bond of Iniquity?*—Slaves to all the *Follies*, the *Vanities*, the *Pleasures*, and *Pride of Life?*—And what should *restrain* them? Not *this Faith* most certainly! For this, not being a *Faith of the Operation of God*, can have no *supernatural* or *divine Influence* over them.—It not being a *divine living Principle* inspired by the *Spirit of God*, can

can never give any *spiritual Life* to a Soul *dead in Sin* ; nor enable it to *act according* to the *divine spiritual Gospel* of the *Lord Jesus!*

So *wide* is the *Difference* between a *Faith*, which none but *God* can *inspire* ; and a *Faith*, which every *proud Pharisee* may lay claim to!

And therefore, is it surprizing, that *such a Believer* should be for ever complaining of *falling short* in Duty? This, he certainly *will* and *must* do, whilst *Conscience* retains any Power of *reproving.*

However, his *Comfort* is, (provided he *can* take *Comfort* in it) that *Christ* is *his Law-fulfiller ;*—that *Christ has kept the Law for Him!*—Consequently, it may well be asked,—What would this *weak Believer* have? Would he *keep*, for instance, the *Ten Commandments?* For *what Reason?*—Has not *Christ kept* them *for* Him? Or does he think he can keep them *better* Himself?— Why then should he indulge this *legal Spirit?*— However, so it is ; that every time, *such weak Believers* break one of the *divine Commands*, their *Conscience* is apt to fly in their Face, and make them quite *miserable!*

One would think, that some of the following *Scriptures* had fastened upon their Minds!—" If ye love me, says the blessed Jesus,
" *keep my Commandments.* He that hath *my*
" *Commandments, and keepeth them*, he it is
" *that loveth* me.— If a Man *love* me, he will
" *keep my Words.*—He that *loveth me not*,
" *keepeth*

"*keepeth not my Sayings.*—Herein is my Fa-
"ther glorified, that ye bear *much Fruit.*—
"If ye *keep my Commandments,* ye shall *abide*
"*in my Love*; even as I have kept *my Fa-*
"*ther's Commandments,* and *abide in his Love.*
"—Ye are my Friends, if ye *do whatsoever*
"*I command you.*"—St *John* xiv. 15, 21,
23, 24. Ch. xv. 8, 10, 14.

"By this," says the beloved Disciple of *Christ,* "we know that we *love* the Children "of God, when we *love* God and *keep his* "*Commandments.* For this is the *Love* of "God, that we *keep his Commandments*; "and *his Commandments* are not *grievous.*"
—1st Epist. v. 2, 3.

St *Paul* declares, that "we are the *work-* "*manship of God, created in Christ Jesus* "*unto good Works*; which God hath before "ordained, that we should *walk in them.*" He prays that the *Colossians,* "might be ena- "bled to *walk worthy of the Lord unto all* "*pleasing; being fruitful in every good Work.*" And he directs *Titus,* "*constantly to affirm,* "that they which have *believed in God,* "might be *careful to maintain good Works* (a)." And only to mention one or two Passages more, "The Dead were judged every Man "*according to their Works.* Blessed are they," says the *Alpha* and *Omega,* "That *do his* "*Commandments,* that they *may have right to* "*the Tree of Life.* I will give unto every "one of you, *according to your Works.*—
"Hold

(a) Ephes. 2. 10. Colos. i. 10. Titus iii. 8.

"Hold that faft, which thou haft, that *no* "*Man take thy Crown.*" Revel. xx. 13. Ch. xxii. 14. Ch. ii. 23. Ch. iii. 11.

But now, is it poffible for a *ferious Chriftian*, to attend to thefe *awful Declarations*; (even though he knows he muft be *faved* of *mere Grace only*), and not feel a *deep Concern* for fo frequently *falling fhort* in the difcharge of his Duty?—And yet a very *ferious Chriftian* declares;—" that *Believers* will never "live *comfortably*, till they fee the *Law dead* "*and buried!*"

I had much rather they could fee " the "*old Man dead and buried!* The *whole corrupt Nature crucified*; and *the Body of Sin* "*deftroyed; that fo*, they might *not henceforth ferve Sin!*" But on the contrary, be " *dead indeed unto Sin*; *but alive unto* "*God, through Jefus Chrift our Lord!*" Rom. vi. 6, 11. For I fear there are but *too great* a Number already of thefe *comfortable Believers* in the World! Such *ftout-hearted* ones, as feldom betray a *legal Spirit*, when they have violated any Branch of the *divine Law*. But who being *hardened through the Deceitfulnefs of Sin*, are able to fin on, with much *Peace* and *Tranquillity* of Mind!

Believer, whoever thou art, let me intreat thee, *not to be afraid of humbling thyfelf before God, under every Deviation from the divine Commands*. Otherwife, *thy Spirit will grow more flack and remifs; and thy fleepy Negligence will make thee pay dear, for having*

been

been more afraid of *a legal Spirit,* than *of violating the Law of God!*

Indeed, when Men are taught, that "though God is *able* to save them from the "*very being* of Corruption, *now* as well as "*in Heaven*; but that it is not *his Mind* "and *Will:* And that he will *send Death to* "*kill Sin*:"—I say, when they are thus taught, can *such Doctrines* tend to stir them up—"*to cleanse themselves from all Filthiness* "*of the Flesh and Spirit*; *and to perfect Holiness in the Fear of God* (a)? Or to use *all* "*Diligence to add one Grace to another*; and "even *to abound* in them; that so they may "be neither *slothful* (b), nor *unfruitful* in "the Knowledge of *our Lord Jesus Christ* (c)." So far from it; that without more *Light* and *Power,* than *such Doctrines* have any tendency to inspire,—the *Believer* will only sink deeper into the *sleep of Sin* and *eternal Death:* And may *contentedly* wait for *Holiness,* till both *Holiness* and *Heaven* are shut up from him!

But surely, whatever tends to *slacken* our *Zeal and Diligence* in seeking after *universal Holiness* (which implies *universal Obedience*) can never proceed from the *Gospel of Christ!* And further, when God promises his People, to "*cleanse them from all their Filthiness and* "*all their Idols:*—To *give them a new Heart* "*and a new Spirit:*—To *put his* [holy] *Spirit within them*; and *to cause them to walk*
"*in*

(a) 2 Cor. vii. 1. (b) ἀργες.
(c) 2 St Pet. i. 5, 8.

"*in his Statutes*, and *to keep his Judgments,* and *do them* (a);" Can'ft thou, *Believer,* imagine, it is *time enough,* to part with *all thy Filthineſs,* and *all thy Idols,* when thou comeſt into the *Regions of Holineſs?* Or that it will be *ſoon enough* to receive the *holy Spirit* to cauſe thee to *walk* in the *divine Statutes,* and to *keep* and *do* the *divine Judgments,* —" when *Death is ſent to kill Sin?*"—Believer, reflect attentively on thy *high Privileges!*

Thou art called to be " *an Habitation of God, through the Spirit;*—to be *ſpiritually united to Chriſt;* and to have *Chriſt dwelling in thy Heart by Faith;* and *out of his Fulneſs to receive, and Grace for Grace.*" Thou art alſo called to " *a Fellowſhip with the Holy Ghoſt;* to have *the Kingdom of God ſet up within thee,—even Righteouſneſs, and Peace, and Joy in the Holy Ghoſt:* And even *to be filled with all the Fulneſs of God* (b)!"—How can'ft thou therefore imagine,—that *it is agreeable to the Mind and Will of God,* that the *Kingdom of the Devil* ſhould alſo continue within thee, till *Death comes to deſtroy it?*

Art thou not called to " *put off the old Man and his Deeds;* and *to put on the new Man, which after God is created in Righteouſneſs*

(a) Ezek. xxxvi. 25—27.
(b) Ephes. ii. 22.   St John xv. 4—7.   1 St John i. 3.   Ephes. iii. 17.   St John i. 16.   2 Cor. xiii. 14. St Luke xvii. 21.   Rom. xiv. 17.   Ephes. iii. 19.

"*teoufnefs* and *true Holinefs?*" Ephes. iv. 22—24. But can the *old Man* be thus *put off*; and yet *live and rule* in thy Soul? Or doft thou think it *needful* he fhould *live* there, as long as thou *liveft* upon Earth, in order to *make* and *keep* thee *humble*? Be affured, that one *powerful Ray* of *divine Grace* will make thee more *humble and holy*, than poring upon *thy Corruptions*, for twenty Years together! God gives us a Sight of them to *humble* us; but this will not *cleanfe* us. Dream not therefore of any *Neceffity* for thy continuing a *Leper*.—*Chrift* came on purpofe to " *make* " *an End of Sin, and to bring in everlafting* " *Righteoufnefs.*" He is now *willing* and *able* to *cleanfe* thee of *thy Leprofy!*—Therefore oppofe not thy *Unbelief* to his *Will* or *Power!* Be not *faithlefs*, but *believing:—All Things are poffible to him that believeth.* Believe therefore; and the *Victory* is *thine!* Take heed, *Believer*, left thy *Unbelief* prevent *many mighty Works* from being wrought in thy Soul! However, be ftrictly careful, that thy *Faith* be of the right Kind;—*Faith of the Operation of God; working by Love,* and bringing forth all *the Fruits of Righteoufnefs*; for thou art called *to be filled with them.* Moreover, pray earneftly, that *the Love of God may be fhed abroad in thy Heart by the Holy Ghoft*; and that thou mayeft *love Him,* with *thy whole Heart,* and *Soul,* and *Mind,* and *Strength*(*a*); and that

(*a*) Dan. ix. 24. St Matth. viii. 2, 3. St John xx. 27. St Mark ix. 23. 1 St John v. 4. St Matth. xiii. 53. Col. ii. 12. Gal. v. 6. Phil. i. 11. Rom. v. 5. St Mark xii. 30.

that thou mayest be *armed* with the *whole Armour of God*; and then fear not but *Satan* and all his *Host will fly* before thee! "*Be thou* only thus *strong in the Lord, and in the Power of his Might* (a)." But let not the great *Apostle* of the *Gentiles* prove a *stumbling-block* to thee! He was no more *set* for *thy Fall*, than his *great Master*. Both indeed have unhappily proved *so* to many! But it was entirely *their own Fault:* And therefore, I intreat, that thou wouldst not increase the Number!

Do not say, that " the *Apostle Paul*, even " after he had gloriously preached *Christ* for " above *twenty Years*, was, by his own Con- " fession,—*Wretched*, and *Carnal*, and *sold* " *under Sin* (b):" And then conclude, that " it would be *Folly* 'and *Presumption* in thee, " to expect to be less *wretched*, less *carnal*, " or less *sold under Sin*."

This *wretched Logic*, which it is to be feared has ruined Thousands of Souls, will but hold thee faster in the *Chain* of thy *Sins*; and consequently keep thee much longer out of the *glorious Liberty of the Children of God!* It has indeed the *Authority* of the great St *Austin*; but what Pity is it, that he ever altered his *first Thoughts!* For after his Mind was *heated* (or as the learned Dr *Whitby* expresses it, after it was *soured*) by the *Pelagian Controversie*, his Sentiments were all changed
for

(a) Ephes. vi. 10—18.   (b) Rom. vii. 14, 24.

for the worſe (*a*). Before this *fatal Period*, he *expreſsly* and *frequently* ſays, that the *Apoſtle* was only *deſcribing* "*a Man under the the Law,' before Grace.*" And elſewhere he thus mentions his Opinion,—"The *Apoſtle* "ſeems to me in that Place to have *taken* "*upon himſelf*, the *Perſon of one*, who was "*under the Law* (*b*).—Of the *ſame Senti-* "*ments* appear *all the Fathers* before St *Au-* "*ſtin*; and all the *Greek Commentators* (*c*)." And happy had it been for the World, had St *Auſtin* never been *provoked* to *change his Opinion!* Since, as the ſame learned Dr *Whitby* obſerves, " it gave Occaſion to *the* "*perverting* the *plain Senſe* of the *Apoſtle* (*d*)."

However, our *ingenious Author* "eſteems "it as a Proof that the *Apoſtle* was there "ſpeaking of *himſelf*; becauſe he mentions "*himſelf Thirty-eight Times.*" Let us therefore examine, whether the *Number of Times* can *prove* this *favourite Point*.

For ſuppoſing St *Paul* had repeated theſe Words

___

(*a*) Poſt autem Animum erga *Pelagianos* acerbatum, omnia in pejus, pro more mutavit.

(*b*) Deſcribitur Homo ſub Lege poſitus ante Gratiam. —*Liber expoſ. quat. propoſ. ex Epiſt. ad Rom.*—Quo loco videtur mihi *Apoſtolus* transfiguraſſe in ſe Hominem ſub Lege poſitum —*Ad Simplic. Mediol.* Lib. I.

(*c*) Eſt porro inſuper notandum Patres omnes ante *Auguſtinum* exiſtimaſſe *Apoſtolum Paulum* à commatte ſaltem decimo quarto hæc ſcripſiſſe, non de ſeipſo jam renato ſit Commentatores *Græci* omnes.

(*d*) See the learned Dr's *Stricturæ Patrum*, and his *Commentary* in loc.

Words,—" *through my Lye (a)*"—even *forty Times*, inſtead of *Thirty eight*;—would our *ingenious Author* have concluded, that the *Apoſtle* really meant a *Lye of his own?* Or ſuppoſe, that St *James* had, *as often* ſaid — therewith (that is, *with the Tongue)* " curſe " *we Men (b),*" would this be any *Proof*, that he deſigned to include *himſelf?* Or if St *Peter* had ſaid *fifty Times (c),*—" *when we* " *walked in abominable Idolatries,*"—yet, who would have concluded from thence, that he had *himſelf* been an *abominable Idolater?*— And laſtly, ſuppoſe that our *holy Lord* had, even *five hundred Times*, called the *Bread, his Body*, and the *Wine his Blood*; would this in the Opinion of our *Author*, have been *any Proof* of *Tranſubſtantiation?* I durſt ſay it would not. Therefore the *mere Repetition* of a Word or Sentence can neither help us to the *true Meaning*, nor make the leaſt Alteration in it.

However, this learned Writer thinks he has found a *Demonſtration*, from the viiith of the *Romans*, Verſe 2, that St *Paul* did certainly ſpeak of *himſelf* in thoſe Parts of the *ſeventh Chapter* —Let us view it. " *The Law of the* " *Spirit of Life in Chriſt Jeſus*," ſays the Apoſtle, " *hath made me free from the Law of* " *Sin and Death*," Rom. viii. 2. This, it ſeems, is a *Demonſtration*, that this very Apoſtle was *then carnal* and *ſold under Sin!*

How

(*a*) Rom. iii. 7.   (*b*) St James iii. 9.
(*c*) 1 St Pet. iv. 3.

How *differently* does the *same Demonstration* affect *different Persons!* I have always taken *this Verse* as a *plain Demonstration* of just the *Contrary!* And that I may not be thought *singular* in it; I shall mention the Sentiments of a truly learned and pious *Divine*, who must be esteemed (at least in the present Case) to be a very *unprejudiced* Judge.—

"To suppose," says the late Reverend Dr *Doddridge*, "the *Apostle* speaks all these "Things of *himself*, as the *confirmed Christian*, that he *really was* when he wrote this "*Epistle*, is not only *foreign*, but *contrary* to "the *whole Scope* of his Discourse, as well as "to what is *expressly asserted*, Ch. viii. 2. (*a*)."

Let us next proceed to what our learned Author tells us, concerning *imputed Righteousness.*

"*This*, he affirms, the *Apostle* has not "*scrupled* to mention *eleven Times* in one "Chapter, *Rom.* iv." They, who can discover *imputed Righteousness* mentioned *eleven Times* in that Chapter, have, I must confess, a. superior *Eye-sight* to mine —I can only find in *that Chapter*, the *Apostle* speaking, *six* or *seven* Times, of *Faith imputed for Righteousness*;—that is, *Faith imputed* or *reckoned* as the *Mean* or *Instrument* of *Justification*, as our *own Church* expresses it in her *Homilies* (*b*); because *by*, or *through Faith*, we

(*a*) *Family-Expositor*, on *Rom.* vii. 7. *Note a.*
(*b*) Part II. p. 258, 259.

we are *justified* (*a*); that is, *by*, or *through Faith*, we embrace the *pardoning Love of God*. And therefore, when St *Paul* varies his *Phrase*, in this *Chapter*; and mentions—" God im-
" puting Righteousness;" Verse 6. and " that
" Righteousness might be *imputed* unto them
" [the *Gentiles*] also;" Verse 11.—what can the *Apostle* mean, (if we suppose he talks *consistently*) but that " God *justifies* or *pardons*
" a Sinner *through Faith?*" There being no other Way of *Justification* for *Jew* or *Gentile*. Thus is the *Apostle* quite *consistent* and altogether of *a Piece*: Nor is *imputed Righteousness* (in our learned *Author's Sense*) so much as *once* mentioned in the *whole Chapter!*

But let us, in the last Place, take Notice of this Gentleman's *Criticism* on the Particle ἐν (*b*), in St *Peter's second Epistle*, Chap. i. Verse 1. and which he insists should have been translated—*in*.

In the first Place, he is too good a *Scholar* not to know, that the *Greek Particle* ἐν (like the *Hebrew Beth*, to which it answers) has *various Acceptations*; and therefore it does not *necessarily* signify—*in*.—However, let it be translated—*in:* and let the *Sentence* be thus rendered,—" Faith *in* the Righteousness of
" our God and Saviour;"—yet it will not afford the least Encouragement to the *Unrighteous*, (whilst they *live unrighteously*) to
rely

(*a*) Rom. v. 1.
(*b*) It is indeed in the *Piece* ἡς: But this is a Mistake of the Printer.

rely upon *imputed Righteousness!* For what is *Faith in* that *Righteousness of our God and Saviour*;—but *Faith in that Justification,* which *Christ,* by *his Blood* has purchased for us; and which, *by Faith,* we receive from God? And what is this, but St *Paul's Justification by Faith?*—And is it any wonder, that St *Peter* should *agree* with him?

Believer, if thou hast any true Value for thy Soul, take heed of what is commonly called, *imputed Righteousness!*—Be assured that neither St *Peter,* nor St *Paul,* ever preached it. For can'st thou imagine, whilst St *Paul* bids thee,—" *to work out thine own
" Salvation with Fear and Trembling*; *to
" deny ungodliness and worldly Lusts*; *and to
" live soberly, and righteously, and godly in this
" present World* (a)." Can'st thou imagine he should *tell* thee,—" thou *need not* do either: For *Christ* has done *all!*"— Or when St *Peter* commands thee,—" to *give Diligence to make thy Calling and Election sure:
" Nay,* to give *all Diligence,* to add *one
" Grace to another*; and even to *abound in
" them* (b);"—can'st thou get leave of thyself to suppose,—that he would *teach* thee,—
" that *nothing* was *necessary* for *thee* to do;
" but only to *plead* the *Obedience* of *Christ,*
" who had already performed the *whole* for
" thee?" Therefore let me advise thee if thou art a Stranger to the convincing Power of the Spirit,

(a) Philip. ii. 12. Titus ii. 12.
(b) 2 St Pet. i. 5, 10.

Spirit,—seek for that Holy Spirit, through *Christ*, to work powerful Convictions in thy *Heart* ;—to apply the *atoning Blood* to thy *guilty Conscience* ;—to seal up the *pardoning Love* of God to thy Soul, by a *divine Faith* ;—to make thee a *new Creature in Christ Jesus* ; and to enable thee to " *be fill-ed with all the Fruits of Righteousness, which are by Jesus Christ unto the Glory and Praise of God* (a)."

Thus, *Believer*, may Thou and I " *grow in Grace, and in the Knowledge of our Lord and Saviour Jesus Christ* (b)!" May we " *take up our Cross daily, and follow Christ* (c)!" May we *forget*, with the great Apostle St Paul, " *those Things, which are behind, and reach forth unto those Things, which are before; and press toward the Mark, for the Prize of the high Calling of God in Christ Jesus* (d)!" May we thus, through the all-powerful Assistance of the *Holy Spirit*, be enabled to " *fight* the *good Fight of Faith:*" —and then, through the *alone Merits and Mediation* of the *Lord Jesus*, may we " *lay hold on eternal Life* (e)!" And may the same *divine Blessings* be the Portion of *every serious Reader*, for the Sake of *Him*, who " *tasted Death for every One* (f):" And therefore

---

(a) Phil. i. 11.   (b) 2 St Pet. iii. 18.
(c) St Luke ix. 23. (d) Phil. iii. 13, 14.
(e) 1 Tim. vi. 12.   (f) Heb. ii. 9.

[123]

therefore to *Him*, with the *Father and Holy Spirit*, be ascribed *all Honour*, *Praise*, *Power*, *Might*, *Majesty* and *Dominion*, both now and forever. *Amen (a)!*"

(*a*) Rev. i. 5, 6. Ch. v. 12, 13. Ch. vii. 10.

F I N I S.

———

E R R A T A.

Page 9. Line 19. for *carnol* read *carnal*.
—40. in the Note, line 6 for *Rev*. ii. 15. read *Rom*. xi. 26.
—102. in Note (*b*) for συἸγένειαν read συῖγένειαν.

Published by the same Author.

I.

A VINDICATION of Mr *LOCKE,*

FROM THE

CHARGE of giving ENCOURAGEMENT to *SCEPTICISM* and *INFIDELITY,*

And from several other Mistakes and Objections of the learned Author of the *Procedure, Extent, and Limits of Human Understanding.*

In SIX DIALOGUES.

Wherein is likewise enquired whether Mr *Locke*'s true Opinion of the Soul's Immateriality was not mistaken by the late learned Monsieur *Leibnitz.*

Humani nihil à me alienum puto. TER.

II.

A SECOND VINDICATION OF Mr *LOCKE.*

Wherein his Sentiments, relating to *Personal Identity,* are cleared up from some Mistakes of the Right Reverend Dr *Butler,* late Lord Bishop of *Durham,* in his Dissertation on that Subject; and the various Objections raised against Mr *Locke,* by the learned Author of *An Enquiry* into the Nature of the *Human Soul,* are considered:

To which are added,

REFLECTIONS on some PASSAGES of Dr *Watts*'s Philosophical Essays.

Censure is the Tax a Man pays to the Publick for being eminent. Lord *Bacon.*

www.ingramcontent.com/pod-product-compliance
Lightning Source LLC
Chambersburg PA
CBHW020057170426
43199CB00009B/317